When Getting Along Is Not Enough

When Getting Along Is Not Enough

RECONSTRUCTING RACE IN OUR LIVES AND RELATIONSHIPS

MAUREEN WALKER

TEACHERS COLLEGE PRESS

TEACHERS COLLEGE | COLUMBIA UNIVERSITY

NEW YORK AND LONDON

Published by Teachers College Press, 1234 Amsterdam Avenue, New York, NY 10027

Library of Congress Cataloging-in-Publication Data

Names: Walker, Maureen (Psychologist), author.
Title: When getting along is not enough : reconstructing race in our lives and
    relationships / Maureen Walker.
Description: New York, NY : Teachers College Press, 2020. | Includes
    bibliographical references and index. | Summary: "Using anecdotes from
    her psychology practice, Walker provides a way for educators and social
    service professionals to enter into cross-racial discussions about race and
    racial relations. She identifies skills that are essential for repairing the damage
    wrought by racism and provides exercises to stimulate group conversations
    in staff development, classrooms, and workplace training"— Provided by
    publisher.
Identifiers: LCCN 2019036742 (print) | LCCN 2019036743 (ebook) | ISBN
    9780807763384 (hardcover) | ISBN 9780807763377 (paperback) | ISBN
    9780807778241 (ebook)
Subjects: LCSH: Intercultural communication. | Race relations. | Racism. |
    Stereotypes (Social psychology)
Classification: LCC HM1211 .W36 2020 (print) | LCC HM1211 (ebook) | DDC
    305.8—dc23
LC record available at https://lccn.loc.gov/2019036742
LC ebook record available at https://lccn.loc.gov/2019036743

ISBN 978-0-8077-6337-7 (paper)
ISBN 978-0-8077-6338-4 (hardcover)
ISBN 978-0-8077-7824-1 (ebook)

Printed on acid-free paper
Manufactured in the United States of America

With gratitude and in loving remembrance of my mother,
Mary Louise Walker
1922–2007

Contents

Acknowledgments

If there is one thing I know to be true, it is that we most truly come alive and grow when we are in good connection with others. Writing this book has allowed me to dwell in the heart of growth-fostering relationships. When I met Karen Propp, almost 20 years ago at Harvard Business School, I had no idea that she would be the *Sherpa* who would guide me through this passage of my life's work. I knew her first as a writer-editor whose expertise was helping business professionals translate their technical skills and financial models into accessible prose. As my developmental editor, Karen brought her intellect, her patience, and her absolute insistence on precision in the face of paradox and multiple truths. Hearing my computer ping with one of her "I-think-you-should-say-this-more-clearly" emails helped me to become a more effective truth-teller. If we turn to physical trainers to develop muscle strength, I would say that Karen is a mind trainer who pushed me in developing my mental agility. I am deeply grateful to Karen for sharing with me her patience, persistence, and professionalism.

I once heard a writer describe his partner as his "accessory cerebral cortex." When I think of my colleague Alice Moses's contribution to this book, the word "accessory" is a glaring understatement. Alice brought order to what I called a "morass" of text and tangled citations. Not only did she offer her exquisite research skills; she shared her clinical insights, thus helping to bring abstract concepts to life.

In commenting on the history of Relational-Cultural Theory (RCT), throughout this book I have mentioned the colleagues and scholars who have facilitated my clinical development over the past 30 years. What I did not say is that these women are also lifelong friends who have supported and challenged me in the *doing* of relationships, not just the theorizing about relationships. Before I met Judith (Judy) Jordan, I was poring through her prodigious writing on topics ranging from new conceptualizations of self to cultural trauma. I am deeply grateful for her support as our RCT luminary, teacher, and friend.

When I first heard Amy Banks talk about the neurobiology of friendship, I was transfixed. Here was a psychiatrist whose brilliance was not muffled by arcane polysyllabic words that once spoken are quickly forgotten. Egalitarian to the core, she used her words and her expertise not to intimidate or impress, but to illumine the mysteries of our everyday relationships. Amy has a bias toward action and a penchant for the concrete. When I told her I was ready to write this book, her first words were "Let me show you how I wrote my proposal."

I am also grateful to S. M. (Mike) Miller, brilliant scholar, tireless social justice activist, and husband of the late Jean Baker Miller, the psychiatrist who helped me to reframe my understanding of relationship as an ontological imperative. When I met Mike years ago, I was speaking at a convening of activists committed to economic justice. Mike has long insisted that RCT scholarship belongs on the street, where it can play a role in healing the wounds of the world. His words have taken root, not only in my work but in burgeoning scholarship, action research, and social justice initiatives across multiple disciplines.

Of course, an effort of this kind is hardly possible without the loving support (and tolerance) of family. I am the proud and grateful mother of two wonderful human beings: Angela Patrice Shenk and Walker Louis Sands. I admire them both for their creativity, quick-wittedness, intellectual agility, and passion for justice. Thank you for sharing those qualities, your unstinting support, as well as your clarity about what matters for generations to come. My son-in-law Dr. Gregory Shenk is scientist, teacher, and father par excellence. Gregory is the person I could text at midnight and ask where I might find research about some relatively obscure idea. Within minutes, he would offer five or six sources, with promises of more to come in the morning. Thank you for sharing from your deep wells of knowledge and doing your very best to keep us all intellectually honest.

Then, of course, there is Bill (William the 3rd) Larkin. In 1992, Bill invited me to co-facilitate Beyond the Barrier dialogues, the core component of his antiracism ministry as a member of the Paulist Fathers. Much of what I have learned about cross-racial and intraracial dialogue came out of those gatherings at parish retreats and conferences across the nation. Little did we know that our journey would lead to a soul partnership. Before we were married, Bill wrote a poem with the lines:

Racism has left us weak and wasted on the shore;
Come, my Sister, let us cross over to the other side.

Crossing over to the other side has allowed us to grow together in territory that is fraught with isms and schisms of many sorts. He has been my mind–heart reader, and when necessary, my moral whisperer when the path of least resistance seemed to be a descent into disconnection. I am forever grateful that he is my husband, co-journeyer, and friend.

It is impossible for me to talk about anything I have ever achieved without acknowledging the blessing of having been born into the life of Mary Louise Walker. My mother used to write "papers," usually on some religious theme, which I was then tasked to read (or recite from memory) during special Sunday programs or service club meetings. In today's parlance, her "papers" might be called blogs. Although she never had the privilege of attending high school, she trusted her mind to discern wisdom and her voice to speak truth. To my mother, for being my nurturer and my Muse, I am forever grateful.

Introduction

On a steamy July morning in the 1980s, I sat in an auditorium with over 100 other civic leaders and business professionals to participate in a race relations workshop in Macon, Georgia. The session was led by Richard Keil, then pastor of St. Peter Claver Catholic parish and founder of the Tubman Museum. Richard mentioned in his brief opening remarks that race is working on us at all times, whether we're thinking about it or not. Then came his facilitation prompt: Tell a story about your best and your worst experience with a person of a different race. That was it: no icebreaker, no big lecture, no Kumbaya. Instead, he sat and waited for us to rummage through our memory banks in search of a story suitable for telling in mixed-race company.

I imagine we were all slowly starting to realize the challenge of following such simple instructions with a modicum of authenticity. All of us had gained some measure of public recognition in our professions, prerequisite for membership in the assembled group. We were well practiced in "just getting along" across racial lines, maintaining appropriate boundaries (read: distance from each other), and putting our best face forward. In other words, we were prepared to get through this little exercise in racial amity, and then move on with the rest of life. But that's not what happened.

One participant, a White gentleman perhaps in his forties, started telling a story about growing up on a plantation-like farm in South Georgia. As a boy he grew up with Black servants of various sorts, but he was especially fond of an old sharecropper whose family had been attached to his family for generations. Although he expressed a kinship-like affection for the sharecropper, he liked to tease and harass him. He knew the old man was afraid of snakes, and one day as sport, he and his friends threw snakes into a ditch the old man was digging—just to see the old man scramble and cry. As the story went on, the gentleman recalled being summoned home from college to attend the funeral of the old sharecropper. That's when I witnessed the previously self-contained gentleman beginning to visibly shake. We all listened as he recalled looking into the casket. He had known this old man all his life, but only as a digger of ditches, planter of Silver Queen corn, and the object of mean jokes. However, on that July morning as he told his story, wracked by tears, he realized that the day of the funeral was the only time he had ever seen the old man wearing clean clothes. Lying in his casket, the sharecropper was finally shed of the grime-encrusted overalls that marked his debased status, not only in the family, but in the Southern social order. Gazing upon the corpse, the White gentleman caught a glimpse of the sharecropper's fuller humanity.

I have little doubt that over the years my fellow workshop participant had come to regret the snake-throwing incident as a mean, boyish prank. However, it was not until that July morning some decades later that this crusty, hard-bitten Southern conservative began to see how race had shaped his vision of humanity—his own and that of the sharecropper. Perhaps he was stunned at the moment by the degree to which their mutual affection and closeness had been trapped inside the stratified racial system in which they both lived, a system underscored by their differences in dress. Perhaps he was also stunned by the tragic irony that death could bring a dignity to a Black man that had been unattainable in life.

While most of us (fortunately!) have no such dramatic moments to recall, our own imagination of who we are and can be has been constrained by the practices of race in America. I say practices because race is cultural ideology in action: It is something we *do,* not what we are, nor who we might become. Race is how we design and execute our institutional, commercial, and political systems. It is how we embody our relationships with each other, even when—perhaps *especially* when—we are not giving it any conscious thought.

Growing up in the racial apartheid culture of the American South in the 1950s and '60s meant learning how to do race from a very early age. Although I was enrolled in 1st grade well after the 1954 Brown v. Board of Education decision had declared "separate but equal" schools unconstitutional, racial segregation was a defining feature of all of the schools I attended through 12th grade. One operational translation of that feature was that my classmates and I did not receive any brand-new books until we reached the 5th grade. Prior to the day the crisp new dictionaries arrived, cast-off books and hand-me-down desks were unremarkable facts of getting an education while "colored." Those worn and sometimes outdated books and scuffed and sometimes broken desks were enactments of racial ideology; specifically, they signified our status—who we were supposed to be—in the rank ordering of human worth.

Much of my work as a young professional in school systems and hospitals involved addressing the wounds of racial stratification. It was not until I began studying the work of critical race theorists such as Janet Helms and William Cross in my doctoral studies that I began using an academic framework to understand how racial identity shapes and shifts our imagination of human possibility. As a doctoral intern under the guidance of my mentors Drs. Melba Vasquez and Sally Grenard-Moore, I was introduced to a new feminist theory that was then called the self-in-relation model. Propagated by pioneering psychiatrist Jean Baker Miller, the theory proposed that the capacity to participate in healthy connection, rather than the commonly lauded capacity for self-sufficiency, was the hallmark of psychological maturity. Furthermore, Miller and her coterie of colleagues contended that chronic disconnection was the primary source of all human suffering.

Most often, chronic disconnection is conceptualized as interpersonal wounding or disruption; for example, adverse experiences associated with family dysfunction or violations in intimate relationships. However, as racial identity theory and self-in-relation began to coalesce in my work, another compelling question started to take shape: What if the culture itself is the agent of chronic disconnection? How does experiencing our subjectivities through the interpretative framework of racialized inequality shape our imagination of who we think we are? Moreover, how do the cultural enactments of racial inequality shape our capacity to form healthy, authentic relationships within and across racialized categories? Over the past three decades, the self-in-relation model has evolved into Relational-Cultural Theory, the framework that provides the conceptual underpinning of this book. What started as an academic question during graduate school is now the core of my life work.

Arriving in Boston in 1991 to work as a psychologist at Harvard Business School, I intensified my involvement with the clinicians associated with the Stone Center Counseling Service at Wellesley College. At the Stone Center, I began meeting regularly with the founding scholars of the theory: Jean Baker Miller, Irene Stiver, Judith Jordan, and Janet Surrey. A guiding mantra of our work together was taken directly from an often quoted Miller dictum: A healthy connection is one in which all participants have an opportunity to grow. We grew together as did the theoretical model. During our weekly meetings, it became apparent that we needed to emphasize the role of culture in psychological development. Sometimes we sat in Miller's living room excitedly finishing each other's sentences. At other times, we presented new ideas at the Stone Center Colloquia, or we gathered around conference tables at national symposia to test ideas and share insights about creating and sustaining healthy connections in a culture marred by chronic disconnection: disconnection enfleshed by the isms endemic to social relations in American culture.

When Getting Along Is Not Enough offers an opportunity to use relational practices drawn from psychology to transform our consciousness and ways of being in our culture. Although we have learned to use race as a mechanism of disconnection, we can unlearn those cultural habits. Using Relational-Cultural Theory (RCT) anchoring relational practices such as disruptive empathy, mindful authenticity, and dynamic mutuality, we can remake the meaning of race in our relationships and clear pathways to a new imagination of who we can be together.

The first half of this book explains race as an organizing dynamic in American culture, and how it impacts our ways of being in relationship, from the most intimate or enduring to the most ephemeral or institutional.

The first chapter, "The 'It' Without a Name" examines race as a nameless dynamic that operates in ways that are simultaneously blameless and shameless. Chapter 1 through Chapter 5 discuss the practice of racial stratification as a rank-ordering of human worth, a reality that simultaneously shapes our implicit associations and explicit behaviors. Chapter 2, "When the Culture Hurts," addresses the inherent contradictions in the claim of post-racialism. Chapter 3, "Race and Place: What's Power Got to Do with It?" focuses on belonging, the cultural expectations and practices that define who can safely be in what space.

A central tenet of RCT is that all psychological theory or stories of human development are necessarily concerned with questions of power and powerlessness. Power and powerlessness shape the experience of being human, no matter where the subject is located in the rank-ordering system. To survive a culture predicated on the stratification of differences, one must become adept at disconnection—from oneself and from others, however "others" might be defined. To that end, Chapter 4, "Mascots, Missionaries, and Other Illusions of Power-Over," explicates the function of what we in RCT call "power-over," reified and presumably permanent inequality in relationship. Power-over in relationship gives rise to racialized strategies of disconnection, practiced inauthenticity to exert unilateral control in relationship or to mitigate personal harm in relationship. Chapter 5, "Sticks and Stones and Words That Hurt," delves into experiences of social pain and the many guises of modern-day racism. Given that race is a relational dynamic, it morphs into any form necessary to protect the legacy of racialized inequality.

In Chapters 6 through 9, I focus on three anchoring relational skills for personal transformation and cultural healing: disruptive empathy, mindful authenticity, and dynamic mutuality. Following the basic premises of RCT, in Chapter 6, "Disruptive Empathy: Beyond 'I Feel Your Pain,'" I position "self" as a metaphor that includes multiple and sometimes conflicting narratives about race, narratives that we enact consciously and unconsciously on a daily basis. Chapter 7, "Mindful Authenticity," outlines the principles and practices that enable honest and growth-fostering conversations about race. In this chapter, I reframe "keeping it real" as being present and courageous in face of the multiple truths that emerge when the participants encounter each other with thoughtful vulnerability, cultural humility, and active curiosity. The relational anchor highlighted in Chapter 8 is "Dynamic Mutuality," the sine qua non of shared power in relationship. Given the premise that we come to know who we are through action in relationship, this chapter emphasizes the practices that support transformation in relationship. In other words, dynamic mutuality is that relational skill that helps us to move beyond the rigid boundaries of certainty and comfort in order to embrace what we need to learn as well as what we need to teach. Chapter 9, "Say It Isn't So . . . and Other Race-Card Games," goes directly after the linguistic ruses deployed to deflect, derail, or otherwise discredit conversations about race. In this chapter I describe the ideological force field that generates these games, as well as the specific forms these games might take. When confronted with race-card games, even the most agile raconteur may be rendered "speechless." Knowing the forms and function of these game patterns helps to counter that outcome.

In Chapter 10, "Nine Rules for Remaking the Meaning of Race," I do exactly that. We need what I call "rules of engagement" to counter an inherited American cultural legacy that mires our sense of who we can be in conflictual narratives of purpose and possibility, often leaving us not only disconnected from each other, but unmoored from our own moral anchors. That is, the narratives we have inherited from our cultural forebearers cast difference in the binary terms of better than and less than, more deserving and less deserving. Consequently, the narratives we hold to be true about ourselves (who we think we are) are often oppositional and predicated on distorted images of people we perceive to be different from ourselves (who we are *not*). Furthermore, neuroscience research tells us that when we encounter someone we perceive to be different, we are more likely to default into using the part of our brain that objectifies and relies on abstraction rather than experience to learn and grow.

In addition to the rules, I also identify some of the typical silencers, linguistic strategies that thwart movement toward understanding and authentic engagement. Having rules of engagement helps us counter forces that dispose us toward withdrawal and disconnection. Some of these will be on-the-spot practices that you can do with your imagination and inside your own body. Others will require ongoing reflection, preferably with the help of others.

The final chapter, "An Enlarged Vision of Human Possibility," offers a reminder that we are continually creating our narratives of human possibility. We are on a shared journey toward realizing our ultimate interconnectedness. We are not all the same, nor are we on the same journey. To paraphrase the wisdom of activist Audre Lorde (1984), the fact that we are from the American crucible of racial stratification does put us on a shared journey. The relational practices described in this book can anchor and enlarge our vision of shared humanity.

Ten years ago, when I first envisioned a book about healing racial divides, I wanted to call it *Revolutionary Hope*. This title resonated with me because I believed disordered power relations that define racial stratification create hopelessness on both sides of the inequality. To practice hope would be to resist, to subvert the power-over practices that leave us alienated and afraid of authentic connection. Much has happened culturally and politically in the years that have elapsed between envisioning this book and its hard-won reality to give its mission even more urgency. Today, three other reasons are uppermost in my mind. *First*, we are no longer able to pretend that racialized hostilities are a thing of the past. We can longer protect our liberal, genteel sensibilities by soft-pedaling what we witness all too often—most horrifically, the recent White man's murdering of nine Black worshippers in a sacred space. The veil has been torn; our illusions are shattered, and social "niceties" won't reconstitute them.

Second, the glaring racial divisions following the November 2016 elections is fast dissipating any pretense of cross-racial civility. We witness it at international border crossings and in grocery stores. We're seeing the emergence of what comedian Aziz Ansari calls "the lowercase KKK movement, or casual white supremacy." People are now emboldened to give voice to previously smoldering racialized resentments. While some are lucky to be partially protected by class and other sociocultural circumstance, for others this resentment consigns existence to that liminal space between life and death. I like to imagine that most of us are stunned by this upsurge—these outbursts of anger and hatred. Perhaps if there is any positive aspect to this situation, it is that we are forced to let go of numbing denials; we have to contend with a new normal: While we have made some progress, it is not nearly enough to undo the soul-scarring legacy of chronic racialized disconnection.

Third, in some sense, we have been stunned out of the complacency of "just getting along." However, the problem with being stunned is that we don't know what to do. We have been shocked out of our moral ambiguity. We are feeling the sharp edges of that political fence we've been straddling while trying to make nice with everyone. We now know that if we are not part of the solution, we're part of a festering problem. We are anxious—fearful that one misplaced word will torpedo any possibility of an authentic and caring relationship with another human being. We feel betrayed by the whitewashed mythologies and the illusory promises of liberty and justice for all. We get tongue-tied; we shrink back from relationship for fear of losing all hope of relationship. In this climate, it is small wonder that race talk typically devolves into some version of inauthentic posturing or recycled platitudes. Authentic connection is avoided, and vacuous symbolism stands in for meaningful transformation.

I offer this book as both an invitation and a pathway to transformation. When Jean Baker Miller wrote the groundbreaking *Toward a New Psychology of Women* in 1976, her aim was to bring to light long-suppressed perspectives, perspectives without which we are left with a truncated imagination of possibility. My aim in this book is to give voice to suppressed narratives—narratives that enlarge and elaborate our vision of the purpose of human-mattering. Now is the time for us to shed the life-limiting imagination bequeathed to us by a racially stratified culture. Now is the time for all of us to seriously ask ourselves the questions: Who do *I* think you are? Who do you think you are? This book is offered to help us on a shared journey of possibility, one in which we ask: Who, together, might we become?

CHAPTER 1

The "It" Without a Name

How can we work on race relations if nobody can define what race is?

—comment made by a training consultant from
People's Institute for Survival and Beyond

How does it feel when "what's going on" is race? How does it look? More important, when race is "what's going on," how does it shape the answers to questions such as *who am I*, and *what is my place in the world?* Sometimes when race is going on, it looks exactly like this.

On a crisp November morning, a 15-year-old African American boy is making his way to school. He suddenly remembers that he left the protractor he needs for geometry class on the kitchen table. No problem. He has to walk past a large chain grocery store that is two blocks from his school—the kind of store with shelves stocked with school and office supplies. Upon entering the store, he heads straight to the school supplies aisle and begins searching for the right tool. While he is scanning the shelves, a White assistant store manager approaches him and asks to search his backpack. He hands over the backpack and watches while the manager spreads the contents of his bag on the floor, presumably looking to find a stolen item. When nothing is found, the student purchases a protractor, and walks the final two blocks to his school.

The year was 1995. It was the end of the school day and the end of my workday when I heard this story. My son and I were seated at the dinner table when he reported the incident to me, not so much as an accusation against the store manager as an attempt to make sense of what happened. In some sense, he was trying to figure out how he *should* feel by gauging my reaction. He knew he was African American in a hometown with a 90% White population. He knew that his classmates made regular stops in the store before walking the final blocks to school. *What if they saw him being searched?* He knew that the manager was a person with authority, even if he didn't exactly know the extent or the meaning of that authority. He knew that things could get worse if he refused to submit to the search.

In the days immediately following, I requested a meeting and contacted the store manager as well as the corporate officer in charge of Human

Resources. (I also contacted the police chief of our town to report what seemed to be *at best* unorthodox loss prevention practice.)

Three weeks later, we (my son, my husband, and I) sat with the assistant manager, his immediate supervisor, and the corporate personnel officer to discuss the incident. The assistant manager looked flummoxed. Searching my son was his way of protecting the inventory (hence, profits) of the store. Now he was being reprimanded by his higher-ups in front of strangers. As he sat head-bowed and flushed, the store manager and personnel officer offered profuse apologies, criticized his judgment, announced that his aberrant behavior would be noted in his personnel file, demanded that the assistant manager apologize, and assured us that the incident was not racially motivated. After the end of a 90-minute meeting with the adults doing most of the talking, my son piped up with this observation: "You have said repeatedly that *it* was not about race. If it wasn't, can somebody please tell me what the *it* was that prompted my being searched?"

I tell this story to illustrate that insisting on the absence of race as a motivating factor is to suggest some consensual understanding of what race is. Of course, no such understanding was available to guide the conversation in that meeting room, nor is one available to guide the course of our interactions in everyday life.

A BRIEF SURVEY OF RACE (AS AN ESSENTIALIST CONCEPT) IN AMERICA

Now almost 25 years later, incidents such as these still happen: Race is still going on and remains hard to decipher. Race sits like a cipher in the midst of our relationships. Although it is central to what we call our identity, it is hard to define and explain. There has been, however, no lack of trying. Indeed, beginning in the late 17th century, race became a legally codified aspect of American identity (Higginbotham, 1978). (I am using America in a colloquial sense—as if it is synonymous with the United States.)

Beginning in the late 17th century, Virginia legislators created increasingly stringent laws to codify race, thereby distinguishing between indentured servants of European descent and persons of African descent who would become chattel slaves for life (Higginbotham, 1978). These laws in effect created "Whiteness" as a divide-and-conquer strategy to separate enslaved Africans from landless laborers of European descent (Kendi, 2016). Subsequent legislation focused on the uses of race up through the 20th century, from the three-fifths compromise to determine representation in the United States Congress to the anti-miscegenation laws determining the boundaries of marriage and inheritance status.

It was not only the legal professionals and legislators who attempted to settle the meaning of race. In fact, every cultural institution, including theology, medicine, education, and social science joined in this essentially

American pursuit of meaning. According to Boston University professor Phillipe Copeland (2018), "racial taxonomies function primarily as decision models that determine who gets what and what they can do with it." A survey of these institutions will illustrate this point.

Medicine

In the field of medicine, the 19th-century physician Samuel Cartwright published *The Diseases and Peculiarities of the Negro Race* (1851/1967), an article in which he offered his insights not only on the variety and symptom patterns of "Negro diseases," but on the prevention and treatment options of these afflictions prevalent among enslaved populations. Noteworthy among these illnesses were *Drapetomania*, a disease that manifests as a desire to run away from home, and *Dyaesthesia Aethiopica*, with symptoms such as "disrespect for the property rights of others, a tendency to slight work and to raise disturbances with overseers" (Thomas & Sillen, 1972, p. 2).

In the 20th century, no less a personage than the eminent Carl Jung contributed his insights on the relational implications of race. In an address to the 1928 Psychoanalytic Conference, Jung stated: "The different strata of the mind correspond to the history of the races. The Negro has probably a whole historical layer less than the white man. Black primitiveness so infects American behavior in general. What is more contagious than to live side by side with a rather primitive people? The cause of repression can be found in the specific American complex, namely to the living together with lower races, especially with Negros" (Thomas & Sillen, 1972, pp. 13–14).

Theology

Like other significant cultural practices and institutions, religion played an important role in conceptualizing race. Continuing the philosophy of Aristotle, American theologians have attempted to justify slavery and racialized exclusion by extending ontological arguments regarding the origin and significance of racial categories. In Aristotelian logic, natural slaves were persons born to be the property and tools of others with no agency of their own. For example, in the antebellum South, slaveholders hired Christian ministers to instruct slaves about the morality of their enslavement, complete with warnings about the dire consequences of trying to escape their God-ordained condition. The so-called curse of Ham was commonly used as a theological explanation for the existence of racial designations (Haynes, 2002). Inasmuch as blackness was the signifier of the curse, this biblical account also functioned to justify anti-Black racism and enslavement.

Similarly, 18th- and 19th-century theologians appropriated passages attributed to the apostle Paul in the New Testament of the Christian Bible. Particularly useful for this function was Ephesians 6:5, which exhorted slaves to obey their masters not only with "fear and trembling," but with "singleness of heart" (Powery & Sadler, 2016, p. 116). Although the church's role in racializing personhood has shifted since the days of antebellum preaching, Dr. Martin Luther King, Jr., observed that the institutional church remained one of the more racially segregated spaces in 20th-century American culture (King, 1960). Rather than leading with a theology of racial separation or anti-Black racism, conservative religious organizations affirm White supremacy through institutional policy and practice. Some of the groups that exemplify this trend are the Moral Majority, Focus on the Family, and the Religious Roundtable.

Education

Because of its dominance as a socializing function, the notion of race has played a major role in shaping American education policy and practice. Legal prohibitions against education for people of color as well as the subsequent "separate but equal" education practices for Blacks and Whites are well-known facts of American history. Less well-known are the lived experiences of persons seeking to become educated under those policies.

Take for example the story of Heman Marion Sweatt. A postal worker and civil rights advocate from Houston, Texas, Sweatt sought and was denied admission to the University of Texas School of Law in 1946. After refusing to attend the hastily established law school at the Texas State University for Negros, Sweatt was eventually allowed to enroll in classes at the flagship university, so long as he sat in a separate space (Burns, 2010).

Although the 1954 Brown v. Board of Education decision mandated the dismantling of separate but equal education "with all deliberate speed," the practice persisted into the 1960s. For example, it was common practice for the state of Georgia to fund postgraduate education in the North rather than allow Black students entry into graduate education programs at the University of Georgia (Pratt, 2002). (In my own family, New York University was a favorite destination.)

Social Science

Of course no racialized practice is complete without substantiating research and ideologies. Enter the combined force of Harvard psychologist Richard Herrnstein and political theorist Charles Murray to corroborate the heritability theory of intelligence (1994), most famously proposed in 1907 by geneticist Sir Francis Galton. In their well-known work *The Bell Curve* (1994), Herrnstein and Murray present data supporting the thesis that social policies, including those that address Black–White achievement gaps in education, must reckon with the fact that intelligence is largely a function of genetic endowment. Notwithstanding their claim that "the quest for human dignity" was the primary motivation for their research, their conclusions are consistent with earlier hypotheses that compensatory practices in education are doomed to be ineffective given the genetically determined cognitive limitations of Black people (Jensen, 1969).

Law, medicine, theology, and social sciences: The unifying premise across the practices and pronouncements of these various disciplines is an essentialist conceptualization of race. The underlying presupposition is race as an immutable category grounded in scientific (or quasi-scientific) fact and legal logic. Race, according to this system of logic, is a thing, a noun, a checked box that signifies incontrovertible social and political consequences.

Let me acknowledge that due to increasing cultural sophistication, few people would publicly define race as a wholly biological condition. In spite of resurgent efforts to pinpoint racial heritability factors (Plomin, 2018; Plomin, Owen, & McGuffin, 1994), most academic discourse makes at least a deferential bow to environmental factors implicated in racialized variability. The research by scholars such as Turkheimer (2000) and Nisbett et al. (2012) has moved the conversation many steps forward in the right direction. Further, even in informal settings, the more culturally sophisticated responses to the "what is race" question emphasize the sociopolitical aspects of racial categorization.

However, as we face the conundrum of race in the 21st century, we become aware that while the academic, legalistic, and theological discourse about race may be enlightening, it does little to help us navigate the everyday complexities of racialized interactions. And let's face it: Many (or most?) of our everyday interactions are racialized, whether it is a casual airport encounter with a stranger, a coaching session with an underperforming student, or an intimate conversation with a family member.

If the other person is someone whom we see as racially different from ourselves, there are those thoughts, wishes, or impulses lurking behind the scenes of the encounter: things we dare not do or say for fear of offending or being offended. Worse would be an unintentional linguistic blunder that sparks open conflict or taints the relationship with smoldering resentments that go unspoken and unresolved. The same could happen with someone whom we see as racially similar: We run the risk that misunderstandings, interpretations, and character judgments might complicate an otherwise comfortable encounter. Additionally, we may be prone to make presumptions about shared values and experiences with persons we identify as "members" of our racial tribe.

THE COMPLEXITY OF EVERYDAY RACIALIZED INTERACTIONS: JO AND THE CLERK AT THE CONVENIENCE STORE

A White friend whom I will call Jo told me about an incident that still haunted her, years after the encounter occurred. She was on a road trip, headed back north from Disney World, when she and her family stopped to buy gas at a convenience store. As Jo picked up potato chips and other road trip "necessities," she enjoyed friendly chatter with the clerk behind the counter, another White woman. She learned that the woman was the day-shift manager, a confidante of the store franchise owner, and was responsible for hiring and supervising other employees.

At some point, the conversation turned edgy, as the clerk started talking about "the kind of colored people" she hired, including their typical family structure, level of ambition, and pliable demeanor. Before Jo could gather her wits and redirect the conversation, the clerk called in one such employee, a specimen so to speak, for Jo to examine. Jo introduced herself; shook hands with the man, and exchanged brief pleasantries before he went back to his duties.

In about 30 seconds, the awkward encounter was over, but not before Jo noticed a knowing, "see-what-I mean" glance from the clerk. Jo felt herself turning icy and resentful toward the clerk, and very troubled by her inability to respond to the situation in a way that felt consistent with her politically progressive ideas. (*It was after all a short chance encounter with a woman she would never see again. How much effort was it worth?*) We can only imagine what the clerk made of the Northern woman who suddenly became rude and abrupt before leaving the store.

This kind of encounter, though remarkable in Jo's experience, is not uncommon. What is common is that our definitions and ideas about race don't always translate into effective relational action. Furthermore, like Jo, we may be left with lingering resentments and self-recrimination after a disappointing interaction. Like Jo, we may feel unmoored from the conceptualizations that shape our sense of who we are in the world. Although we might casually check a racial category box on some administration form, the check in the box is a static definition, one that does not help us tell fuller truths about our personhood as they emerge in our relationships with others.

Racial identifications are inescapable; sensate experience is the starting point. Claims to color-blindness notwithstanding, we see ourselves and others as members of racial groups. However, to tell the fuller truths of who we think we are, we must be willing to explore how race functions in our lives.

RACE AS A RELATIONAL DYNAMIC

When we get trapped in the checked box with static definitions, it is usually because we are focused on the form, not the *functions*, of race in our own lives, as well as in the lives of others over the course of American history. Because our personal narratives are shaped by our experiences as part of a collective national identity (i.e., American), it is important to think of race or racialized experience as a relational dynamic. It is a dynamic constituted by institutional and ideological practices that function to rank order human worth.

Considerations regarding human worth are marked by personal and institutional responses to questions such as these:

- Who belongs here?
- Who deserves access to particular resources and relationships?
- What are the acceptable boundaries of behavior, and how do those boundaries shift over time, person, and circumstance?
- Who can be trusted to perform this function?
- Who is deserving of dignity and respect?

These questions are more than academic abstractions. Our personal and collective responses are manifest through everyday relational experience, from the disparate availability of resources (e.g., food, healthcare, police practice) across neighborhood communities, to which jokes we find funny.

Furthermore, the responses to these ontological questions shape human experience on an everyday basis, whether the questions are consciously articulated or not. Most often, they are not consciously articulated, an issue we will explore later. They are inextricably interwoven with other, more intimate ontological questions:

- Where do I belong?
- Whom can I trust?
- What do I deserve?
- What is possible for me?
- How will I love and be loved?
- Do I matter?

The evolving responses to these questions are integral to our sense of self as members of a human and specifically American cultural community. As one friend, a proudly patriotic, post–World War II immigrant from Hungary put it, "I didn't know I was White until I became an American."

In this sense, race imprints the construction of our personal narratives. It functions less as a description of difference than as a stratifier of worth and belonging. Although the salience of race may vary across contexts, the rank-ordering function remains invariant. In other words, race means more than just "looking different" from each other. It is an interactive mediator of other cultural markers, sometimes described as intersectionality (Cole, 2009) and simultaneity (Holvino, 2010).

I think of intersectionality as carrying many cultures in one body. For example, when I describe myself as an African American, female, heterosexual psychologist, I am representing the experience of embodying four distinctive cultures. I might also use descriptions such as age or religion. The point is this: Each of these markers carries emotional and political significance of culture. That is, in addition to providing instantaneous explanations of how life works, they signify differential power and value. Simultaneity refers to the phenomenological reality that multiple identities may be operative at the same time, with the salience of each influenced by the context.

Irrespective of phenotype or immigrant status, participation in the American narrative forces a recognition of the polarity that defines the rank-ordering function of the racial taxonomy: White superiority and Black inferiority. Social anthropologist Karen Brodkin (1996, 1998), George Lipsitz (1998), and historian Noel Ignatiev (1995) offer brilliant analyses on the stratifying function of race on everyday participation in American life. Brodkin (1996), for example, positions African Americans at the core of not-Whiteness, a designation against which Whiteness and a more fluid range of not-quite-White and not-bright-White have been constructed. She particularizes this theme in her 1998 publication *How the Jews Became White Folks*. Lipsitz (1998) elaborates on the economic ramifications of a racialized society, while Ignatiev (1995) addresses immigrant assimilation and asks how an oppressed race, specifically Irish Catholics, becomes an oppressing race in America. An epigraph in his book, *How the Irish Became White*, uses a quote attributed to Frederick Douglass: "The Irish who at home, readily sympathize with the oppressed everywhere, are instantly taught when they step upon our soil to hate and despise the Negro . . ." The overarching thesis of each of these writers is that immigrants to this country learn to shed ethnic identification in order to capture the benefits of American Whiteness.

A comment made to me by a young Ghanaian banker seems to reflect Brodkin's premise that African Americans represent the core inferiority of not-Whiteness. As an up-and-coming professional residing in Brooklyn, he was reluctant to allow his younger brother to join him in the United States. He feared that his busy schedule would not allow him to monitor his younger brother's friendships and keep him away from the basketball courts where those African American kids hang out with their droopy pants. Although other immigrant and ethnic groups also resided in his neighborhood, his specific concern was protecting his brother from the tainting influence of those "Black American kids."

NOVEMBER MORNING REDUX AND THE "IT-NESS" OF IT ALL

Let's go back now to that November morning when a White assistant store manager decided to conduct a search on an African American boy who was standing in an aisle looking at school supplies. Until the manager asked to search the backpack, everything about the scene was perfectly ordinary. Every person was doing exactly what he should have been doing: The manager was walking the aisles surveying activity and inventory; my son was trying to prepare for geometry class. There were other shoppers in that grocery store as well, no doubt doing what early-morning shoppers do: looking for bread, or coffee, or a bottle of milk. To the best of my knowledge, none of them got searched.

The whole tenor of the situation changed when my son's presence in the aisle signaled "danger" to the store manager. The words "mind if I search your backpack?" may seem innocuous to some people—perhaps even polite. Except for one thing: They never should have been spoken. The fact that they were spoken by an adult with authority to a 15-year-old high school student communicated something far more menacing than a simple request: for starters, "I think you are a thief"; "this is how we deal with people who steal."

I can imagine that many other thoughts were racing through my son's head, but to avoid greater humiliation and endangerment (i.e., police officers being called), he saw no other option than to submit. All of this happened before the school bell rang. Now let's freeze-frame the moment when he watched the contents of his backpack being spread on the floor for any gazing shopper to see. In those moments of physical and existential threat, how might he have responded to the question, Who do you think you are?

At no point during the "debrief" process did the store manager seem ill-intentioned: He seemed like a young man who wanted to do his job well, impress his bosses, and make his way up the management chain. At no point did anyone in my family accuse him of racism. When we pressed for an explanation for what had happened, it was the corporate manager who first mentioned race to explain what had *not* happened. That said, it is important to wonder what motivated the young assistant manager to see a young Black boy dressed for school and think "criminal."

As the mother of the Black boy, I wonder whether or not the "mind bugs" were embedded in the organizational culture. Despite his supervisors' effort to isolate the assistant manager as a bad employee, I saw an earnest (though misguided) young man who had been trained by the culture to react as he did. It was for this reason that I invited the police to participate in solving a community problem, a problem with which they were embarrassingly familiar. It was in our town that a few years earlier that a Black Boston Celtics player was wrestled to the ground because someone had reported him as looking like a bank robber (Associated Press, 1990). The police chief responded to my request with a letter stating his apologies and his commitment to helping the store conduct "loss prevention" training that did not involve profiling young Black boys as shoplifters.

SO WHO DO YOU THINK YOU ARE?

Constructing a narrative of our lives is an ongoing experience. It is how we make sense of our meaning and purpose in life. Just as our American narrative has no coherence or credibility without reckoning with our racialized history, our personal narratives too must include an honest reckoning with the meanings and functions of race in our lives. It's not easy to do. Yet it is important to do, perhaps now more than ever.

REFLECTIONS

Recall an incident that made you feel uncomfortable because race may have influenced what transpired. (This could be an incident in which you were directly involved, or one that you witnessed or was reported to you.) How did you make sense of what happened? Who helped you process the incident? Did the meaning of the incident shift over time?

CHAPTER 2

When the Culture Hurts

We can't go on like this. We have to heal this wound, or we will never stop bleeding.

—Atticus Finch in *To Kill a Mockingbird* (Lee, 2006/1960)

Following the election in 2016 of our first visibly mixed-race president of the United States, social pundits rushed to declare that his inauguration ushered in an era of post-racialism. From this standpoint, the election of Barack Obama nullified the argument of race as a viable factor determining American quality of life.

Among the more vociferous proclamations were those by Dinesh D'Souza, a policy analyst who has produced an almost annual stream of publications asserting that not only is racism nonexistent, but that any assertion otherwise threatens the integrity and well-being of the nation (2012, 2017, 2018). As an avowed political conservative and provocateur, D'Souza maintains a polemical stance that may differ significantly from other arguments premised on the claim of post-racialism.

Indeed, it may be said that the post-racialist perspective stems from aspirations deeply rooted in the American ideals: the sanitized narrative of equal justice, fair opportunity, and the inherent dignity of all persons. However, in this era of ever-widening social and economic disparities, fractious politics, and ever-more-visible racial violence, the emptiness of that claim could not be more apparent. Yet, devotion to the idealized narrative persists, competing with the challenging realities that characterize life in 21st-century America.

RACIAL STRATIFICATION

A truthful construction of our personal narratives begins with the recognition that questions about our essential humanity must be answered within the context of an American culture marked by entrenched racial stratification, a rank-ordering of human worth that belies its highest ideals of justice and equality.

This impact of the contradiction—that we want American culture to promote justice and equality while we continue to live in a culture that ranks White people as superior and Black people as inferior—inserts itself in everyday ways. For example, we can't ignore the unspoken "thought bubbles" that pop up like counter-narratives to the pre-meeting banter in our workplaces, especially when the content of those bubbles is filled with words we dare not say in mixed-race company. We may want to contain those counter-narratives, curate our image, and manage the impressions others have of us. Therefore, talking openly about this cultural contradiction may feel like venturing into a relational minefield.

- What if I say the wrong thing?
- What if someone thinks I'm a racist?
- What if someone thinks I'm "playing the race card"?
- At what point does "speaking more carefully" in mixed-race settings constitute avoidance?
- At what point does refusing to be "politically correct" constitute aggression?

It is no wonder that race remains a stealthy presence in our relationships and in our narratives about who we are in relationship. In the 21st century, now more than ever, race remains an "it" without a name.

This may not be a post-racial culture, but haven't things changed? This is a fair question, to which a fair response is a resounding "yes and no!" The contradictory narratives make it difficult to name the "yes-ness and no-ness," but here are three factors that are implicated in our 21st-century racial conundrum.

RACE AND NEUROSCIENCE/YOUR BRAIN ON RACE

Race, Implicit Bias, and Amygdala Hijack

Of all the factors that block authentic conversations, one of the most thoroughly researched is implicit bias (Phelps et al., 2000). We literally can't know what we see, nor can we be aware of our "automatic" reactions to what we see. In those instances, a person claiming "not to see race" is telling the truth. This experience is quite unlike the anxiety-bred strategy of so-called "color-blindness," which we will discuss later.

In their fascinating book, *Blindspot: Hidden Biases of Good People*, Banaji and Greenwald (2013) describe this phenomenon as "mind bugs" that operate outside of our conscious awareness. In other words, just because race is out of mind—presumably the case for the assistant store manager who searched the backpack of a 15-year-old Black boy shopping for a protractor—doesn't mean it's not on the brain. The insights gleaned from research in the field of neuroscience fully illustrate this point. While it is not the purview of this book to thoroughly review those data, it is important to note that our brains store information and memories that are not consistently available to conscious awareness; yet those very memories and stored knowledge may influence our interactions in profound ways.

Using magnetic resonance imaging scanners to map brain activity, researchers have been able to demonstrate that the emotional centers of the brain "light up" when subjects are shown photographs of people they identify as "different race" (Phelps et al., 2000). Many of these studies suggest that negative feelings about Black people may be stored as "mind bugs" in both White and Black Americans.

Under conditions of stress (e.g., stereotype threat, racialized anxiety), the activity of the amygdala in the emotional centers of the brain overrides the prefrontal cortex, which governs the more cognitive functioning of the brain. Daniel Goleman (1995) coined the term "amygdala hijack" to describe this function. Is it possible that the White assistant manager felt threatened or stressed by the sight of a Black teenager in his store and searched the boy's backpack due to an amygdala hijack?

Race and the Implicit Association Test

Meanwhile, Banaji's research led to the development of the Implicit Association Test (IAT), an instrument that is widely used in education, business, and other institutional settings to help individuals measure the association between their concepts and judgments about people they perceive to be different from themselves. Specifically, the IAT measures attitudes about difference that carry emotional valence and that may influence how individuals interact. In other words, this instrument assesses attitudes that bypass conscious awareness.

After taking the IAT as a classroom exercise, a young Haitian American woman burst into my office tearful about what was for her a bewildering discovery: *"I had no idea I could be prejudiced against black people!"*

Her discovery was one that Lawrence (1987) discussed in his *Stanford Law Review* article "The Id, the Ego, and Equal Protection: Reckoning with Unconscious Racism." In addition to describing his inarticulable humiliation as a 5-year-old listening to the story of Little Black Sambo in a kindergarten classroom, Lawrence argues that well-intentioned people pass on their unconsciously learned messages about the inferiority of Black people. A central thesis in this article is that because racist attitudes may exist outside conscious awareness, people create and perpetuate laws that may appear to be "facially neutral" but are in fact "racially discriminatory" (p. 318).

Let me share an example of "facially neutral to racially discriminatory" from the realm of social relations. In the early 1990s, I was invited to co-facilitate a national workshop on multiculturalism in business and organizational settings. In the conversation following the presentation, a White woman commented, with completely earnest and benign intent, that there were no racial problems in her home state of North Dakota because no Black people lived there.

Based on that comment, one might infer that she associated racial problems with the visible presence of Black people, not with the racialized attitude that White people, like herself, may hold. She seemed to have no awareness of the "mind bugs"—attitudes that problematize the existence of Black people in certain spaces. One can only imagine the impact of living or working alongside someone whose very presence is experienced as a potential threat.

Sadly, when undercurrents of such racialized anxiety belie facially neutral policies, the outcome can turn deadly. Even though all candidates (irrespective of race or ethnicity) receive the same training to join the police force, it is Black individuals who are more likely to be victims of police brutality. For example, in Boston, MA, a city whose population is approximately 25% black, 70% of the 15,000 individuals whom police observed, interrogated, or searched were Black (Ransom, 2017). In what has become a spate of extrajudicial killings since 2012, words like "a demon" (Sanburn, 2014) and "large silhouette" (Lockhart, 2018) have been used to justify the killings of unarmed Black victims. What do these tragedies have to do with the brain on race? The officers (and neighborhood vigilantes) have only to "perceive" a threat in order to justify use of deadly force. The threat itself may turn out to be no more than dark skin and a package of Skittles (Benedictus, 2013).

RACE AND THE "DOSE" EFFECT

Given the ambiguities in the present-day racial climate, it can be tempting to relegate racism to the past, an aberration of history performed by unenlightened people. Sometimes also, the insistence that "things have changed" is an attempt to gauge the "dose" effect of racism: How noxious must an incident or encounter be to be described as racist?

Consider this experience through the lens of Oumou Kanoute. Kanoute, a black college sophomore, was eating her lunch in a college common room when she was approached and questioned by police who "were wondering why she was there." With her close-cropped hair and dark skin, Kanoute had been described as a "suspicious black man." In a social media post, Kanoute described the incident in this way:

I am blown away at the fact that I cannot even sit down and eat lunch peacefully. Today someone felt the need to call the police on me while I was sitting down reading and eating in a common room at Smith College. This person didn't try to bring their concerns forward to me, but instead decided to call the police. I did nothing wrong, I wasn't making any noise or bothering anyone. All I did was be black. It's outrageous that some people question my being at Smith College, and my existence overall as a women of color [sic]. I was very nervous and had a complete metldown [sic] after this incident. It's just wrong and uncalled for. No students of color should have to explain why they belong at prestigious white institutions. I worked my hardest to get into Smith, and I deserve to feel safe on my campus. (Oumou Kanoute, 2018)

Kanoute went on to explain that she was originally reluctant to raise an outcry, knowing there were people who wouldn't believe or support her. As it turned out, she was exactly right. In the days following the incident, a *Boston Globe* columnist wrote an opinion piece describing Kanoute's experience as "the racist incident that wasn't" (Jacoby, 2018).

In Jacoby's view, the incident was nonracist because the officer was unarmed, spoke to her politely, and left her in peace. He concluded by characterizing Kanoute's stressful (if not humiliating) encounter as a "minor misunderstanding by a cautious employee was quickly resolved and never escalated into anything dangerous" (Jacoby, 2018). Seemingly, the absence of actual nooses or dead bodies negated any credible claim of racism.

Microaggressions

Clearly, the newspaper columnist's perspective is at odds with decades of research on microaggressions, a term coined by Harvard professor and psychiatrist Chester M. Pierce in the 1970s (Pierce, 1974). The term has become codified in race theory discourse by scholars Derald Wing Sue, Tori DeAngelis, and others. Microaggressions are marked by ambiguity. As DeAngelis (2009) puts it, "they may be so subtle that neither the victim nor perpetrator understand entirely what is going on." Described as "brief and commonplace," microaggressions may be "behavioral, verbal, or environmental indignities" that communicate negative perceptions of people of color (p. 42). (The classic 2010 text by D. W. Sue, *Microaggressions and Marginality: Manifestations, Dynamics, and Impact*, includes a comprehensive glossary of terms to describe these racialized ambiguities.)

Aversive Racism

Amplifying earlier work by Kovel (1970), Dovidio and Gaertner (1986) discuss aversive racism to describe the conflictual experience of White

Americans who possess strong egalitarian beliefs and attempt to dissoci-
ate negative feelings about Black people from their self-concepts, but "who
nonetheless cannot entirely escape cultural and cognitive forces" (p. 6).

Between the extrajudicial killings, whether by vigilantes or the police,
that might constitute "real" racism, and vaguely felt tensions that are classi-
fied as microaggressions, there is a continuum of racialized complexity that
can thwart even the most well-intentioned efforts to bridge the violence and
violations endemic to a racially stratified society.

BEYOND THE BARRIER: RACE DIALOGUES

It has now been more than 3 decades since Wellesley College research scholar Peggy McIntosh famously wrote about what is now called the "invisible
knapsack" of White privilege, and noted its inextricable binding to systematic oppression by listing 50 seemingly benign White privileges such as:
"I can go shopping alone most of the time, pretty well assured that I will
not be followed or harassed" and "I can do well in a challenging situation
without being called a credit to my race" (1988). Similarly, in cities across
the nation, community activists and trainers from The People's Institute for
Survival and Beyond (PISAB) have been encouraging workshop participants
to grapple honestly with the meanings of race in their lives. In these settings
a more basic question arises: For whom is the "knapsack" invisible, and for
whom is it hypervisible?

Taking a cue from PISAB trainers Ron Chisom and Reverend Dave
Billings, my husband and I co-led antiracism workshops in the early 1990s.
These workshops were an offshoot of Black–White dialogues held in the
1980s as part of my husband's Paulist ministry in New York City. In the
retreats and workshops that we called Beyond the Barrier, there were two
questions that invariably ignited a range of intense emotional responses.

Racial Identification

First, participants were asked to group themselves based on their racial identification. As you might imagine, participants start to show the first signs of
hesitation with this request. In one session, a woman with caramel colored
skin and long, sand-blonde hair voiced her frustration about people expecting
her to identify as Black. "After all, my mother was Danish," she insisted.

Another participant, more out of curiosity than to be argumentative,
prodded her: "Are you saying you have no African ancestry?" "Well," she
responded eventually, "my father was black American." Another woman insisted that she couldn't join the White group because she was a Jew.
Again, another participant urged the process along by asking, "How do

other people see you who don't know you're a Jew?" Another participant asked, "How do you act when no one has asked you to describe yourself?"

Usually, all of these participant-generated questions provided valuable content for the ensuing conversations. Once the groups had sorted themselves, the first facilitator questions began.

Ethnicity

This question was easy for the White-identified participants. There was always laughter and stories, often stories about family holiday traditions or recipes handed down through the generations as resistance stories: how the family came to "make it" in American culture. Within this group, the question also prompted conversations about religious cultures (e.g., practicing Judaism).

Since most of these retreats were pre-Ancestry.com or other "roots" inspired enterprises, the conversations in the Black-identified groups were a little less lively. With the exception of those with known immigration histories (e.g., West Indies, Ghana), few of the Black participants had reliable information about their ethnic or national origins. Interestingly, Black-identified participants who could trace their immigration history often took pains to distinguish themselves from Black participants whose ancestors were likely survivors of chattel slavery in America. As a woman from Belize demanded of another Black-identified participant without a clear immigration history: "Don't associate *me* with that mess!"

Fortunately, as the sessions grew in popularity the ethnic diversity of the participants increased; people who identified as Latinx, Asian, or South Asian joined the groups. Typically, if there were two or more people who identified as "other than" Black or White, they formed their own group. At other sessions, participants would join the "race" group with whom they shared more affinity (e.g., some Puerto Rican participants would join the "White" group, others the "Black" group). In general, this part of the session proceeded in a smooth and predictable fashion. Then the tables would turn with the second question.

What Do You Like About Your Race?

This question was easy for the Black-identified group. Anyone walking past the "Black" conversation space was likely to hear raucous laughter, conversations about food, family traditions, music, and even resistance stories. In one session, a young woman who identified as Nuyorikan said: "White people have dinner at 6 o'clock; Puerto Ricans have dinner when the food is ready." Her assertion was met with knowing laughter from the other participants in her group.

If there was a group that identified as "other than Black or White," they would discuss how they felt "positioned" as Americans vis-a-vis these racialized polarities. In some cases, the participants could simply take the path of least resistance and "pass" as White. (In the absence of some extraordinary stressor, such as an unwitting disparagement of their ethnic group, this strategy worked rather well.) For those who could not "pass" phenotypically, the conversation often centered on the daily calibrations required to function within a racialized society. As suggested by Brodkin's 1996 thesis, while they would never be considered "bright white," they could avoid the mark of indelible blackness (p. 475).

Typically in the White-identified group, the question was met with uneasy silence, then sometimes consternation, and often outrage. There was always anger about the question itself. Eventually the White group would begin tentative discussions that centered around two major themes: never having to think about Whiteness or some of the benefits of Whiteness. One White male participant smilingly acknowledged that he was happy that he could make sure his Mexican American wife never got cheated in a car dealership. In another session, a White woman who felt affronted by the question looked at me and said rather pointedly: "I like that at least I don't have to do s*it-loads of stuff to my hair to look good."

Talking About the "It" That Is Hard to Name

Why, you might ask, would we go to such lengths to set up these potentially polarizing conversations? The groupings are purposeful. Irrespective of national origin, phenotype, or political philosophy, racialized polarities are endemic to American culture. Structuring groups along these lines (with ample flexibility for choice—e.g., golfer Tiger Woods's self-designation as Cablinasian, Associated Press, 1997) quickly draws out the conversations about the "it" that remains unnamed but ever operative in less-structured settings. The forced structure may be artificial, but the conversations that develop are not.

Without the structure, the discussions are likely to amble off onto side paths. As Ron Chisom from the People's Institute liked to say: "Among white people, participants will divert the conversation toward classism or sexism—all for the purpose of escapism. No one really wants to talk about race" (personal communication, 1995). The exercise provided safe, even if somewhat uncomfortable, boundaries within which to talk about the "it" that is hard to name.

Shame shuts down conversations, and the disparate experiences with opportunity, access, and privilege engender shame. Admittedly (and certainly in the post–2016 election climate), there are some people who revel in the disparities. However, it is a fair assumption that very few people want to be directly implicated in someone else's oppression. Hence the often angry denials: "I (or my family) never owned slaves!" In other words, *"Don't blame me for the gaping racialized disparities that mark 21st-century American culture!"*

The reaction is exactly right. Finger-pointing and hyper-personalized blaming only serve to exacerbate racialized tensions. In fact, the very nature of systematic or culturally engendered privilege is that it is woven into the fabric of society and is therefore invisible.

SYSTEMIC AND BUILT-IN PRIVILEGE

Let me offer a non-race-related example. In a meeting with my Harvard Business School program administration colleagues and a professor from one of the teaching units, my administrative colleague "Kay" jokingly remarked to professor "Steve" that she was happy to have him in attendance. His presence in the meeting meant that we could have the meeting catered. Professor "Steve" flushed beet-red; he had no idea that system policies (all in the name of fiscal responsibility) generated such a disparity. Steve gently inquired about the justification for the "rule," to which the only real response was "we know the rule, not the reason."

What was interesting about the exchange was that it was not meant to trigger discomfort for anyone, but Steve was visibly embarrassed. He had done nothing wrong. All he knew was that every time he went to a meeting, snacks were available. There was no way for him to know, nor was there any reason for him to assume that the meeting world worked differently for administrative professionals. At the conclusion of the meeting, he joked, "Any time you want to use my name to get snacks, please feel free to do so."

Obviously, the point of this exchange was not to resolve the snacks-or-no-snacks dilemma, but to highlight how systematic privilege functions to foster oblivion regarding advantage. It also reveals the importance of "rules" for groups not similarly served by built-in privilege. For those groups, it is imperative to know which rules cannot be violated.

Second, the notion of built-in privilege stands as a counter-narrative to the notion of individualized meritocracy. In other words, we want to believe that we have earned whatever privileges or social benefits we receive by exertion of our individual will and effort. Anything else is an entitlement, social charity, or worse, a handout. To feel "entitled" to handouts or to receive handouts is a mark of inferiority, hence the effectiveness of Ronald Reagan's fictive Welfare Queen as a racially polarizing political tool.

However, in the 18th-century South, European indentured servants (unlike Black slaves) were entitled to acreage, money, and other resources when their period of indentureship ended. In the 20th century, President Roosevelt capitulated to the practice of White entitlement to earn the support of Southern Democrats for his New Deal legislation. Southern states were allowed to invoke "states' rights" in determining which racial group was entitled to benefits and in what measure (Jones, 1997; Lipsitz, 1998).

In the 21st century, racialized dispersal of resources is evident in every arena of social functioning: education, judicial rights, housing, and health care to name a few. If talking about the disparity between availability of snacks (which in reality no one needed) could trigger mild anxiety, how much more discomfiting is reckoning with the reality that American culture from its inception and throughout its history was built on practices that overtly privileged White American identity. The impulse is to suppress that uncomfortable sensation through avoidance (sometimes accomplished through justification), anger, or aggression.

Suppressed Shame

Let me offer a quick—again non-race-related—example of avoidance. At my place of employment, I once commented on the hypervisibility of custodial workers using cell phones during the workday. I mentioned that on more than a few occasions, I had overheard workers having urgent sounding conversations in a restroom stall or had seen someone going about his work with a broom in one hand and phone in the other. And I *noticed*. Those conversations could look like a distraction—a lack of focus on their assigned duties.

I, on the other hand, was free to pick up my office phone and make doctor's appointments, talk with accountants, or call a friend or relative to talk about *absolutely nothing*, and never run the risk of anyone questioning my focus because of my telephone habits.

When I make this observation (and I have done so now in a number of settings), not a second passes before someone rushes to assure me that I have earned the right to use the telephone as I need or please because of my education, professional attainments, or whatever. In other words, my telephone behavior can be attributed to merit, not to distraction or dereliction of duty. Once a privilege is converted to merit, shame dissipates until the next built-in privilege is called into awareness. Or more likely, shame is suppressed.

However, suppressed shame about systematic privilege or systematic oppression eventually manifests. Sometimes it is experienced as helplessness, despair, or emptiness. At other times, it erupts in expressions ranging from vague antagonism to vivid rage.

Once the suppression begins, we are vulnerable. Our humanity is on the line and we develop elaborate strategies of disconnection that thwart our authentic engagement in relationship. We lose the wherewithal to connect with our own ways of knowing, through sensate experience as well as cognitive-affective awareness. We also become less courageous in our desire to know and be known by others, hence limiting the possibility to experience the fuller truths of our human existence.

TWO MODELS OF HUMAN ENGAGEMENT:
RELATIONAL-CULTURAL THEORY AND RACIAL IDENTITY THEORY

What does it take to let go of shame and expand our imaginations of what it means to be fully human in a racially stratified culture? I first began to engage this question when I was introduced to two models of human development: Racial Identity Theory and what was then called Self-in-Relation Theory.

The premise of Self-in-Relation Theory was that chronic disconnection was the primary cause of human suffering (Jordan, Kaplan, Miller, Stiver, & Surrey, 1991). I also began to read and think about the implications of racial identity as a process of meaning-making, rather than strict categorization (Helms, 1990). The question arising from these two bodies of work seemed inevitable: What happens when human suffering is rooted in culturally sanctioned disconnection? In other words, rather than viewing chronic disconnection simply as an interpersonal event, what if we viewed the culture as an agent of disconnection which, in addition to shaping our narratives about self and others, determined systems of access and opportunity? Furthermore, how would those systems of access and opportunity reflect and reproduce the narratives? (Walker, 1999). The increasing centrality of these questions led to what we now know as Relational-Cultural Theory, named as one of the 10 most influential models of human development (Jordan, 2010; Jordan, Walker, & Hartling, 2004; Miller & Stiver, 1997; Walker & Rosen, 2004).

Relational-Cultural Theory

If you ask any American what it means to be a mature, fully functioning adult, chances are you will hear words like independence, individuation, self-sufficiency, self-control, self-esteem, and so on. These are words that are central to the story of human development—as the story is told by Western psychologies (Freud, 1937; Kohut, 1984).

There are two problems with that story. The first is that it is based on the need for separation. With each successive stage of development (and there is the implication that mental health and maturity should proceed in an orderly fashion, e.g., mastery of one stage and then on to the next), human beings are presumed to have less need for others. At the apex of the process, their locus of control is securely implanted somewhere inside the self, ensuring adequate mastery of wishes, impulses, needs, emotions, and relationships.

While relationships play a major role in this story, their role is secondary and utilitarian. That is, good-enough relationships enable healthy autonomy and independence. In this story, the self emerges with a capital S, actualized, fulfilled, and with enough positive esteem that it can feel really good about itself. When the Self feels good about the Self, it can become an even better Self. The story comes complete with diagnoses and labels for people who somehow fail to demonstrate adequate levels of autonomy and control. Some of the words used to mark this shortcoming are external locus of control or low self-esteem, or maybe just "needy."

You may notice that this notion of a healthy Self resonates strongly with American notions of individual meritocracy and seeds the impulse toward rivalry and competitiveness. The larger problem with this story is that it is literally, biologically untrue. It also sets forth an illusion as the gold standard of human development. From the standpoint of these models, only those humans whose social privilege allows them to sustain the *illusion* of independence can sustain this impossible goal of self-sufficiency.

It is no wonder then that persons who are not systematically privileged are automatically problematized, or worse, pathologized, by what I call these "separated Self" stories of human development. For instance, in early Freudian formulations women were deemed somewhat less evolved, less capable of attaining higher levels of moral development because of the inadequately resolved Oedipus Complex. Notions such as these when never fully repudiated contribute to a range of social ills, not the least of which is the enduring assumption of women as less credible and competent beings (Freud, 1961; Miller, 1984; Schafer, 1974; Slipp, 1993).

What distinguishes the Relational-Cultural model of human development from the "separated Self" models is the premise that humans grow through relationship not for the purpose of independence, but for the purpose of relationship. That is, developing one's capacity to be effective, creative, and productive in relationship is the goal and marker of healthy maturation.

Pioneering psychiatrist Jean Baker Miller (1976) put forth these basic formulations:

- We grow and come to know who we are through action in relationship.
- Because nothing grows by interacting with a mirror image of itself, conflict is both inevitable and necessary for healthy development.
- Chronic disconnection is the primary cause of human suffering.
- The Central Relational Paradox (CRP) of human development is that we are neurologically hardwired to grow and thrive in relationship, and because relationship may be the site of frustration and harm, we are also terrified in relationship.

Chronic Disconnection and the Racially Stratified Culture

The sine qua non of a racially stratified culture is chronic disconnection. Such cultures are characterized by presumably impermeable boundaries:

laws, regulations, and social norms that separate the included from the excluded, the more deserving from the less deserving, and in the parlance of
2012 presidential candidate Mitt Romney, the "givers" from the "takers"
(Jonas, 2012).

Such ontological dualism is the hallmark of racially stratified culture.
The emotional motif underlying such cultures is fear, and racialized conflict
devolves into combat. Hence, a reasonable survival strategy in a racially
stratified culture is to become adept at disconnection, and to do so in ways
that mimic authentic engagement and interaction. We will explore the manifestations and consequences of these strategies of disconnection in later
chapters. Suffice it now to say that they prove inadequate in navigating
the racialized complexities of the 21st century; they also short-circuit any
impetus to expand the relational competencies required for healthy human
functioning.

Racial Identity Theory

If Jean Baker Miller and the founding scholars laid the groundwork for a
"new psychology" of human development now called Relational-Cultural
Theory (RCT), Janet Helms (1990), William Cross (1991), and other scholars of racial identity development theory (Bonilla-Silva, 2014; Helms &
Carter, 1990; Sue, 2015) established the theoretical framework that illuminates how we come to understand who we are as racialized beings.

When I was first introduced to this work as a doctoral intern at the
University of Texas Counseling Center, I felt as if I had found the Rosetta
stone of psychological development. Having long been interested in the impact of race on human experience, I found that the racial identity theories
obliterated the crude categorical descriptions of race to facilitate a more nuanced understanding based on meaning systems and practice. Furthermore,
while much clinical literature and practice focused on "minority" status, the
experience of Whiteness in America remained largely unexamined (Doane
& Bonilla-Silva, 2003). In other words, the nearly exclusive focus on minority status has allowed Whiteness to linger in the shadows, functioning as
the invisible, unarticulated but presumptive norm.

Old habits die hard, so my first forays into the literature consisted main-
ly of trying to pinpoint the stages: Was this or that person in Pre-Encounter
or Disintegration or Enmeshment (Helms, 1990). Deeper reading and experience with the literature helped me to understand racial identity development not so much as lockstep progression through predetermined stages
but as systems of meaning that assume greater or less salience in specific
contexts (Cross, 1991).

Professor and author Beverly Daniel Tatum (1993) offers a brilliant
example of this understanding. In her work with graduate students, she
navigated a compelling exercise that helped them establish a timeline of

racial meaning. The basic question required them to note how their views of themselves as a (insert race) person have changed over time.

MULTIPLE-VOICED NARRATIVES

Encountering the racial identity development literature along with what was then called the "self-in-relation" model of Jean Baker Miller and the Stone Center scholars (Jordan et al., 1991) spurred new questions as well as new approaches to my clinical practice. For example, it was taken as a given that psychological harm ensues when people experience pain or disconnection in interpersonal relationships. Holding the two streams of literature together led me to ask two what-ifs:

- What if the culture is more than a mere backdrop to action in relationship?
- What if the culture itself is the primary agent of suffering and chronic disconnection?

In other words, our sense of place and purpose in the world is shaped not only by formative relationships but by the omnipresent cultural messaging that establishes standards of beauty, goodness, worth, values, and reality. For example, in a racialized culture, a conventional understanding of the word "minority" doesn't apply. It has little to do with real numbers; instead, "minority" marks positioning with relationship to the dominant cultural power irrespective of the actual size of a given demographic. This kind of misnaming contributes to the obfuscations that undergird racial stratification. Moreover, it amplifies socially sanctioned narratives, both inchoate and articulated, that shape how we see ourselves in relationship to others in the world.

These are narratives of disconnection that pull us out of our basic humanity: our hardwired yearning for connection. They offer a very small story of human possibility. As Jean Baker Miller suggested, examining the narratives as told through multiple voices illuminates and enlarges our perceptions. When we open ourselves to the voices of our experience with others, we are better able to know and to courageously call out the "it" that constrains our capacities for authentic engagement with each other. Put simply, knowing how "it" functions to shape our personal narratives enables us to make courageous choices and expand our imaginations of who we can become in the world.

REFLECTIONS

1. Recall when you first became aware of race as a consequential aspect of your identity.
2. How were attitudes and beliefs about race (your own and other people's) communicated to you as a child? How do you transmit messaging about race to younger people in your life?
3. What role does race play in the formation of boundaries around friendships in your life? What role does race play in your life choices regarding education and health care?
4. Respond with one word to this statement:
   When I think of myself as a _____ (insert racial identity) person, I feel _____.

CHAPTER 3

Race and Place
What's Power Got to Do with It?

Our problem is how to help our students appreciate diversity. Why do you keep talking about power!?

—School administrator to consultant

Well-intentioned people often like to talk about diversity. In fact, pride in being part of a diverse group, be it a workplace or friendship circle, is often proffered as a measure of cultural enlightenment. Partly as a result of the various civil rights movements of the past half-century, people who claim different social identities are more likely to interact with each other on a consistent basis. Too often, what we see, however, is only the "face" of diversity: people of different colors, genders, and languages, living and working together in ways that would have been uncommon just 50 years ago. While it makes for a pretty picture, the issues that keep us divided are more than skin-deep. The preferred metaphor for American identity was once the "melting pot"; in the mid-1960s, many diversity trainers shifted to the well-intentioned "salad bowl" metaphor: A little (but not too much) of this and a little of that all mixed together would yield a dish that was at least palatable, if not fully relished. What could possibly be missing from this superficial diversity narrative?

POWER AND POWERLESSNESS IN IDENTITY NARRATIVES

Until we reckon with the experience of power and powerlessness as a defining agent in our identity narratives, the "problems" of diversity will remain unchanged. For example, the school administrator quoted above believed that special workshops about cultural differences was all that was needed to help his students interact in more harmonious ways. Yet issues of difference run deep, and just getting along in a superficial harmony underestimates our human capacity for authentic connection. As author and social work professor Elaine Pinderhughes (1989) points out, deeper connection is not possible without reckoning with issues of power and powerlessness.

Social work professor Dorcas Davis Bowles approached the issue of power from an interesting perspective. In a conversation with graduate students at Georgia State University (personal communication, 1989), Dr. Bowles described her observations of cross-racial differences in parenting practices. Dr. Bowles noticed how mothers of different ethnicities (i.e., White, African American, and Puerto Rican) responded to their children's exploratory behaviors in their pediatricians' offices. She noted that while White mothers tended to support and encourage touching and interacting with objects (e.g., the colorful magazines, pressing their faces against the office aquarium), Black and Puerto Rican mothers tended to inhibit such behaviors. For example, when her toddler picked up an object, a White mother might ask, "What do you have there?" In contrast, she noted that the Black and Puerto Rican mothers were more likely to say, "Don't touch that" or "Come back over here."

I remember finding the contrast mildly fascinating as a metaphor, specifically, the notion of "go forth and claim what is yours" versus "stay in your place." After the talk, I filed the thought away along with other academic curiosities, where it might have remained had it not been for the intrusion of real life.

Here's how it happened.

When my son Walker was in the 2nd grade, he was excited to tell me about a new classmate "Bechou," who had recently immigrated from the Gambia. As a welcoming gesture and to support their budding friendship, I decided to take the boys out for pizza. Walking into the local Pizza Hut was an ordinary experience for Walker and me, but not so for Bechou. He was captivated by all of the sights and sounds and smells, but none more than those he was able to glimpse in the kitchen. "Oh my! What are they doing back there? I must go and see so I can tell my little sister Binneh!" And off he ran to see just what was happening in this strange new place. I'm pretty sure I stood frozen in wide-eyed anxiety before lurching after him to pull him back. What was even more interesting is that my son stood mouth opened, aghast at his new friend's behavior. *Didn't he know he couldn't behave like that in a restaurant?* That's when it struck me. Before Bechou's little impromptu adventure, I didn't think Bowles's research applied to my family. My son was growing up surrounded by high-achieving Black professionals: judges, entrepreneurs, physicians, and professors. In fact, some of my colleagues had taken to calling him "Doc," perhaps to seed in his brain the idea that medical school was in his future. But for all of the explicit messaging and modeling given my son to communicate his limitless options and opportunity, there were implicit messages that were equally strong:

- Avoid being seen as a problem.
- Your behavior must provide proof that you—and people who look like us—belong.
- Color inside the lines: stay in your place.

Just to be clear, had his friend been White, I would have pulled him back as well. But here is my point: I would have done so for reasons of safety, not to protect him (and by extension us) from negative judgments. Before that incident had anyone asked me if I taught my relatively class-privileged child to stay in his place, I might have reacted with indignation. It was that little pizza shop episode that revealed to me how the weight of socially marginalized identity may be transmitted from generation to generation.

In a seminar at the Wellesley Centers for Women, British-Nigerian scholar Amina Mama (2002) defined identity as a construct that carries emotional and political weight. To concretize that definition, let's freeze-frame the scenario at the moment young Bechou started to run toward the kitchen. Imagine for a moment the physical postures of the two boys.

- What is the musculature of unrestrained belonging?
- What is the musculature of constricted belonging?

In other words, how might the physical postures of the two boys express conditional vs. unconditional belonging? For the first 7 years of his life, Bechou had grown up in a country where there was a Black and politically empowered majority. My son, on the other hand, had grown up in a country where Black skin is fraught. Furthermore, how might these physical postures be incorporated into their ideas about who they are in the world? Although it may not be articulated as such, we can begin to see how the emotional and political salience of identity may translate into self-experiences of power and powerlessness.

POWER-OVER

In her book *Toward a New Psychology of Women*, Jean Baker Miller (1976) offered a working definition of power as the capacity to implement, later expanding that formulation as the capacity to induce responsiveness (pp. 5–12). By inducing responsiveness she meant the capacity to have an impact on relationships and the environment. In this definition power is an everyday reality woven into our relationships; however, we typically think about power only when confronted with a situation of inequality.

Here's a brief (and non-race-related) example. We tend to think of physical mobility as a bodily characteristic, perhaps a health concern that is devoid of any political meaning or consequence. If we are "able-bodied," we might decide to go, for example, to a friend's wedding, never once giving thought to whether or not we will be able to get into the venue. Imagine how much more urgent the consideration becomes if we need to wonder if our wheelchair can get through the bathroom door. When the very architecture of the building prohibits free access, the message about who belongs, who is welcome, and whose presence matters is loud and clear. Being able-bodied (so-called normal) means being free to pursue one's purpose (whether enjoying a wedding or going to the bathroom) without having to think about belonging or access. The situation is even more fraught when the person on the "underside" of the inequality is considered problematic—a threat to the comfort or convenience of the so-called normal people.

Miller (1976) came to call such inequality of status and access "power-over," patterns and expectations of inequality that are deeply structured not only into institutional operations but into more personal relationships as well. Can we imagine, for example, a White, American male neurosurgeon at a prestigious teaching hospital being touted as "evidence" of a diverse work force? Interestingly, patterns and expectations need not be ill-intentioned; in fact, they are frequently not.

Power-over relationships happen when one group (or person) can determine who is included and who is excluded within the boundaries of normal. Everyone else becomes "diverse," or a deviation from normal. It is no wonder then that a robust training industry developed first around "tolerating" diversity, then "appreciating" diversity, and finally "affirming" diversity. However the diversity conversation is framed, the issue remains the same: Who gets to be called diverse, by whom, and on what basis? A defining feature of a power-over pattern is the presumed unilateral control of definitions. From this perspective, the poignancy of Du Bois's query in *The Souls of Black Folk* (2005/1903) is almost palpable: "How does it feel to be a problem?"

Not all power differentials (i.e., unequal access to resources and relationships, status, or belonging) can be described as power-over. However, because power-over relationships can look benign and can conform to our expectations of reality, it is important to highlight some critical indicators of power-over relationships. Throughout American history, these five mechanisms have produced the racialized stratification that belies the more preferred "diversity" narratives.

1. ***Difference is stratified into "better than" or "less than."*** Children growing up from the 1970s on are likely familiar with *Sesame Street* Muppet characters who talk about "same" and "different." In these charming scenarios, one Muppet might have pink spots and the other might have green fuzzy hair. At the end of the segment the two Muppets conclude that, although they look different from each other, the differences are superficial (my word, not theirs), and they are essentially the same. In Muppet world, diversity is just diversity. However, in a racialized "power-over" narrative, pink spots and green fuzzy hair are not simply different; one is better than the other, and one is less than the other. The point is that we use the word *diversity* as the Muppets do, but

we do not live in a *Sesame Street* world. We live in a world where difference is stratified.

2. ***Once stratified, the "better than" group is seen as more deserving and more inherently worthy of access to fundamental goods and resources.*** For many years, a popular exercise among diversity consultants was to make a list of stereotypes associated with different racial-ethnic groups. Within minutes, it would become apparent that as the skin tones of the social group darken, the list of negative traits would pile up. Even when "positive" stereotypes were listed for the darker-skinned group, they tended not to be traits that held high value in the larger society. For example, the larger culture tends to value sharp, scientific analyses that are associated with White males more than it values highly proficient dancing skills typically associated with Black people. Claude Steele (2010) has provided prolific documentation indicating how the burdensome weight of negative stereotypic expectation compromises brain power. I have observed that college and graduate students of color often think they must limit their intellectual risk-taking to avoid "being wrong" and deemed unworthy of a seat in the hallowed halls of academia. Ironically, it is just such risk-taking that identifies one as intellectually rigorous, able, and worthy.

3. ***The "better than" group sets the terms of the relationship, including the terms by which the "less than" group may be known.*** Again, there need not be nefarious intent. The power-over differential is set in motion when the "better than" group or trait is exempt from scrutiny. Take another of McIntosh's (1988) observations about the many everyday instances of White privilege: "I can choose blemish cover or bandages in 'flesh' color and have them more or less match my skin." Let's assume that "flesh"-colored bandages were not the result of malign intentions, rather, that no one designing the consumer product considered that flesh might be brown or black, thereby depriving whole populations access to bandages that might more or less match their skin tone. Compared to the seriously harmful consequences of racial stratification, bandage coloring is a somewhat trivial example. I use it simply to illustrate the range of exclusion, discounting, and disappearing that results when one group gets to impose its preferred (or more familiar) narrative on another. Imagine how much more dire the outcome when this function of power-over is operating in the board room, the classroom, or the courtroom.

4. ***In a power-over arrangement, communication functions to distort and confuse, rather than to clarify, reality.*** In some instances, examples of this tendency are laughable, as in statements that predict

minorities will be the majority of the population. It's then a fair question to ask whatever does that mean? What is the minority if it is simultaneously the majority? At other times, the consequences of linguistic distortion are more chilling, as when the phrase "defense of marriage" is actually intended to deny marital status to a significant proportion of tax-paying citizens. A similar linguistic distortion is evident when "national security" is used as a term to camouflage policies that deter the entry of brown- and black-skinned immigrants to the United States.

5. **The sine qua non of any power-over arrangement is the presumption that the inequality must remain permanently intact.** Again, power differentials are not inherently bad. They are in fact often necessary. Whether in an institution or under more intimate circumstances, the differentiation is typically necessary to get things done. An example I like to use is the power differential between airplane pilots and passengers. I think it's safe to say that once we board an airplane, we want the pilot to take charge. None of us would want to engage in a democratic conversation about where we might go and the best route to get there. Therefore, the pilot's job is *to do her job* and take control, which includes getting us safely landed. However, once we are safely on the ground, the differential is erased. The pilot and the passengers should have equal access to bathrooms, lunch counters, voting rights, and the like. It is the presumption of permanency that defines power-over: the presumption that the inequality should be maintained by any means necessary.

The presumed normalcy of permanent inequality is revealed by our expectations regarding who belongs in a given space and how they are to occupy that space. Consider again the readiness of the police to suspect a Black woman student who was quietly reading in a common room at an elite college. They didn't expect a person of color to occupy space at Smith College. Dismantling permanent inequality means we must question expectations about what roles particular groups are allowed in a given space.

Ironically, the presence of exceptions to the presumed inequality often proves the rule. It provides evidence of the power-over pattern. Hence, a few women in CEO roles or a mixed-race male in the White House is often touted as evidence that diversity is once and for all affirmed. However, neither of these situations has dismantled the structural and normative barriers that circumscribe "place" and "power" as a racialized experience.

How do these experiences of power and powerlessness play out in our lives? Let's consider these scenarios taken from real life, reported to me by the people involved.

- After imbibing a few shots at an off-campus bar, a group of college-aged White women decide to pretend to break into cars to see if they can attract police attention. They do. The officers say, "Okay you girls; stop playing around. And get home safely."
- A Latina assistant professor in a predominantly White college is told that her tenure is at risk because students find her "formidable," and her White colleagues question whether she really wants to fit into the existing college culture.
- A Black mother warns her son: "Never talk back to a police officer, even if you know you're right."

RACE, PLACE, AND POWER

A term that showed up with increasing frequency in the summer of 2018 was "white spaces" (Anderson, 2015). It was meant to indicate those places where black and brown people are not expected to occupy, are not welcomed, or are welcomed only under certain conditions. For example, two Black men were arrested while waiting for a friend in a Philadelphia coffee shop. For the "crime" of being there, they were subjected to the humiliation of public arrest (Dias, Eligon, & Oppel, 2018). Although this turn of events was arguably an extreme outcome, it illustrates how racial identity manifests in experiences of power and powerlessness. A White barista felt secure enough in her power and sense of belonging to determine who should and should not be present in that space. Furthermore, she was able to enact that power by enlisting the support of the police officers. Although spaces are no longer racialized by law, the function of exclusion and marginalization may still be carried out through cultural norms and expectations.

Just as identity is a multifaceted and intersectional experience, the experiences of power and powerlessness are fluid and context-dependent. In her book *Connected Teaching* (2019), Harriet Schwartz recounts the experience of a tenured African American professor, a woman with numerous publications and highly regarded in her field. However, her academic bona fides did not protect her from being peppered by mini-assaults from a White female undergraduate who repeatedly suggested that the professor's first authorship was probably due to her collaborators' generosity. In other words, the professor's positional power in the classroom was discounted by her student's assertion of greater social (i.e., racial identification) power. The student could not imagine that her tenured professor was indeed intelligent enough to have earned her status. A similar theme surfaced in a conversation I had with Stanley, an African American academic counselor in a small New England college. He reported that it was not at all unusual to have his credentials questioned by the parents of his White undergraduate students, often stating that they were "paying for their student to have only the best."

These themes of race, place, and conditional belonging can take interesting twists. Parks (2010) describes the role of the "strong black woman" and the "magical negro," people of color who are valued because of their utility to White people. In other words, their agency is enlisted to support the goals, needs, and comfort of their superiors. Unlike Stanley, who was often greeted with skepticism, Parks recalled the excitement of one White father when he learned that the academic dean of the college was a Black woman. Upon meeting her, he expressed his gratitude and relief knowing that his daughter would be taken care of by a "strong black woman." While this might appear at first glance to be a compliment, it is important to at least wonder how the dean's professional role was conflated in the father's mind with "caretaking." His remark, though not ill-intentioned, was nonetheless disrespectful of this Black female academic. It stands as an example of how relational images, interpretative frames that describe, explain, and predict relationship patterns and interactions and expectations, are derivative of what Patricia Hill Collins (2000) calls controlling images.

In her book *Black Feminist Thought*, Collins argues that controlling images are political tools that prove tenacious in their authority to define societal values and expectations. As evidenced by popular fictions, from Margaret Mitchell's *Gone with the Wind* to the 21st-century bestseller *The Help* (Walker, 2012), one controlling image of Black womanhood that proves resistant to change is that of the caretaking "Mammy." Her academic credentials and professional role notwithstanding, the dean's "place" or purpose in this college was to take care of his daughter—an expectation he would hardly have imposed on a male of any race, or a woman of a different race.

The experience of power and powerlessness is about more than hurt feelings, though the chronic stress of hurt feelings takes a toll on the body. Using fMRI technologies, Eisenberger, Lieberman, and Williams (2003) demonstrated that the social pain of marginalization is registered in the same neural pathways as physical pain. To our brains, the pain of social rejection is the same as the pain from physical injury or illness (Banks & Hirschman, 2015). With repeated experience of exclusion, simple anticipation of rejection or devaluation is enough to trigger the stress of social pain and its debilitating emotional and physical consequences.

On a political level, power-over happens when one person or group can force another person or group to live according to the terms set up by the more powerful group. These terms may be set up and expressed through personal interactions or through interactions with institutions. As one African American male put it to me: "Everything we need to survive is controlled by White people. We have to get along with them because they control every system from banking to toilet flushing." (Until the water crisis in Flint, MI, became public knowledge, I thought his statement was a tad hyperbolic.) The point, however, is this: Dealing with the terms and expectations of belonging, not belonging, or conditional belonging may affect health, opportunity, even what we call personality.

Let's go back for a moment to the Ghanaian banker who wanted to protect his brother from the negative influence of African American youths. One day when we were chatting, he said, "My friends from home wouldn't recognize me now because I'm so different. Back there I was seen as popular and cosmopolitan. Here I am a minority."

REFLECTIONS

This is a two-part exercise that may best take place over a few days.

Using the diagram below, list the cultural images, or stereotypes, associated with each social identity and indicate whether the composite of stereotypes results in "better than" or "less than" social power. What real-world advantages are associated with your "better than" identity? What disadvantages are associated with your "less than" identity?

Social Identity	Cultural Images	Better Than?	Less Than?
Race/ethnicity			
Gender			
Religion			
Sexual Orientation			
Physical Ability			
Other			

Now select any one of those identities and imagine (or recall) yourself in interactions with people who share that identity with you. Next, imagine (or recall) interaction with people who do not share that identity. Notice how your thinking, feeling, and behaving may shift across the different interactions. Specifically, notice the degree of congruence between your internal reality (thinking, perceiving, feeling) and your external behaviors.

Reflection: Power Grid

We embody the culture as carriers of stratified social identities. Take a moment to jot down some of the social identities you "carry," the cultural images or stereotypes associated with that identity, as well as the cultural valuing of that identity as "better than" or "less than." This constellation of identities comprises your power grid.

How I Feel about Images Associated with My Racial/Ethnic Group	
How I Typically Interact with Members of My Group	How I Typically Interact with Nonmembers of My Group or in a "Mixed-Race" Environment
Alignment Between What I Feel and What I Do	Alignment Between What I Feel and What I Do

CHAPTER 4

Mascots, Missionaries, and Other Illusions of Power-Over

> We wear the mask that grins and lies,
> It hides our cheeks and shades our eyes,— . . .
> . . .
> Why should the world be over-wise, . . .
> . . .
> Nay, let them only see us, while
> We wear the mask.

—Paul Laurence Dunbar

STRATEGIES OF DISCONNECTION

In Dunbar's poem, the "mask" is a strategy of disconnection, a power-over survivor skill used to gain control of a relationship. Although *strategies of disconnection* are essentially strategies of illusion and deception, they are not always intentional or ill-intentioned. The strategy's goal is to create the illusion of connection by withholding vital parts of one's experience out of the relationship. Because racialized power differentials breed a sense of separateness and wariness, strategies of disconnection may seem to offer the only possibility of relational safety, making us susceptible to being both the perpetrator and the target of these strategies. In other words, we can become adept at hiding from each other in plain sight.

Given what we now recognize as our neurologically hardwired capacity and need for connection, strategies of disconnection may appear to provide short-term safety and advantage, but they are ultimately debilitating, and are the source of much suffering. Interestingly, strategies of disconnection are employed by people who have a desire or a need to maintain connection. In some instances, strategies of disconnection represent a "best effort" to mitigate that suffering, be it physical, material, emotional, or spiritual. In other instances, these strategies may be used to maintain a preferred self-image, one that is socially acceptable or helps the person to gain advantages in a particular relational context. In still other cases, strategies of disconnection are akin to reflexive reactions to the chronic stresses of racialized toxicity. While each of these strategies may be driven by multiple motivations, the overarching goal is control, whether it is to stave off harm or minimize vulnerability or to unilaterally determine the course and outcome of a relational encounter.

Also important to note is that strategies of disconnection are not the exclusive province of persons who hold positional, hierarchical, or social power. These relational patterns may be enacted from either side of the power differential. It might be helpful to think of racialized strategies of disconnection as variations on the themes of internalized dominance and internalized oppression.

INTERNALIZED DOMINANCE

Internalized dominance is a relational–cultural belief system grounded in the lived realities of social inequality. This belief system is the result of an advantaged relationship to privilege, power, and cultural affirmation. The premise of White superiority undergirds the various attitudinal and behavioral expressions of internalized dominance. Just as the belief may manifest in any of a variety of strategies of disconnection, at core is the supremacist, power-over belief system (Walker, 1999, 2005, 2010; Walker & Miller, 2000).

There are two points about racialized belief systems that bear repeating. First, they may be enacted from a position of "less than" or from a position of "better than." In either instance, the point of the resulting strategy of disconnection is to secure power and gain control of the relationship. Second, the beliefs that give rise to the various strategies of disconnection are most often unconscious. Think about it: It is a rare person who would admit to agreeing with people who believe she is inferior. Likewise, it is a rare person who would openly subscribe to a belief that she is inherently better than people from a different racial-ethnic group. Internalized dominance, more often than not, is the result of subtle and systemic miseducation about who has high value in a given culture: who is or who should be the faces and voices of authority on critical social functions.

Quick example: No one, irrespective of race, is surprised walking into a hospital (or bank) to see gilded portraits of White male professional luminaries, directors, and benefactors on display. Remember Banaji's "mind bugs"? It may, in fact, be somewhat unsettling if the subjects of the portraits were predominantly other than White and male. The brain does not readily accept such dissonance. The White male portraits hanging on the wall, subtly reassuring that the institution is working according to expectation, illustrate how internalized dominance slips into the brain unnoticed. Unless someone is intent on investing funds in an institution established, directed, and operated by, say, a multiracial, gender-fluid, linguistically diverse group, the White male portraits would likely prove comforting.

How do strategies of disconnection look in a racialized context? Obviously, these relational patterns may be enacted in many ways. In the sections that follow, I will present scenarios that exemplify some of the typical strategies derived from internalized dominance and internalized belief systems. For mnemonic purposes only, I will tag each scenario with a label that describes the role as it functions to appear connected while remaining disconnected.

Let's start with three roles that emanate from the belief system of internalized dominance.

The Missionary

When Sue was hired as a marketing manager in a fast-growing technology company, she made a commitment to hire "diverse" talent in the various clerical roles needed to support the department's work. She was especially fond of new hire Lexie, a Cape Verdean woman newly graduated from a local technical school. Sue made a point to foster a friendship with Lexie in ways that went beyond a professional manager-mentee relationship. Before coming into the office, she would check to see if she could bring Lexie a coffee or a warm muffin. She also positioned herself as a buffer between Lexie and other supervisors who were often less than pleased with Lexie's work.

The problem was that in the name of "cultural sensitivity," Sue failed to give Lexie the feedback she needed to be successful in the company. She knew that Lexie underperformed on a number of critical tasks. However, she did not want to be aligned with Lexie's critics, many of whom she viewed as racially biased.

Furthermore, Sue came from a family that prided itself on its progressive politics, and she took pride in upholding those social values. She not only wanted to support Lexie, she wanted that support to be visible to those colleagues who viewed Lexie's work with a more critical eye. However, what she found increasingly difficult to conceal was the smoldering resentment beneath her smiles, as she came to believe that Lexie was taking advantage of her "kindness." She noticed that not only did Lexie ignore constructive "suggestions," but she came to expect Sue to agree with her negative comments about other supervisors. Although Sue initially felt flattered to be seen as more "woke" or enlightened than her White colleagues, their "close" relationship did not motivate Lexie to improve her performance.

Again, Sue was not deluded or in any way malevolent; in fact, she was just the opposite. Neither was her supportive behavior inherently wrong. The clue that her management of Lexie was rooted in internalized dominance was found in a *sub voce* thought that she could not ignore: *"After all I'm doing to show my support for her as a diverse person, she should show me more gratitude.*" Although Sue was not ill-intentioned, she was captivated by her own image of herself as a White person who could use her power to "save" a diversity hire.

Had Lexie expressed her gratitude by improving her performance, Sue's relational images might have been preserved. However, Lexie's failure to improve her performance was an affront to the images Sue had of herself and of Lexie. *The relational reality was that Sue was fostering disconnection by withholding parts of herself.* She kept out of relationship those parts that might have helped her to provide the information and oversight that would spur Lexie to make more productive choices, which might have included maximizing the opportunities in that role or finding another job.

The Presumptive Judge

As in many American families, post–Thanksgiving dinner conversation in the O'Rourke dining room in 2008 eventually drifted toward politics. It had been a most unusual two years: In 2006, Massachusetts had elected its first Black governor; and just weeks earlier that month, the United States had elected its first known mixed-race president. Like his siblings, Timothy voted for both candidates. Also like his siblings, he considered himself an unofficial pundit of American politics.

Over the course of the conversation, Timothy pointed out many of the highly publicized actions of the two politicians. These actions ranged from the choice of rental cars that the governor drove, and how his staff chose to decorate the governor's mansion, to the new president's attempt to establish a rapprochement with partisan adversaries in order to enhance his chances of passing health care legislation. Toward the end of the conversation, Timothy concluded: "It's wonderful that these guys managed to get elected. It's about time. But it's clear that they know nothing about power and how to use it."

The Presumptive Judge not only gets to define the content or the standards of engagement, he gets to critique the process, *how* the standards should be met. Timothy may genuinely believe that the days of monochromatic governance should be long gone. However, despite his lack of actual experience in the political arena, he feels qualified to issue global judgments about how two high-profile, successful politicians are executing their duties. He feels perfectly at ease critiquing people who have accomplished what he might never imagine accomplishing. Further, even given his opposition to the two White politicians who preceded the new governor and new president, he never described them as fundamentally "lost in their environment." As politicians who "have no understanding of power," he is essentially judging them as unqualified or incompetent.

Timothy would likely be appalled to hear himself described as a dominator, especially as the practice is described by Beatrice Bruteau (2005). In her treatise on power relations, she argues that the dominator determines "being," in that she or he determines how the dominated will be permitted to "act, behave, and participate in common life" (p. 8). With or without ill intention, Timothy reserved for himself the right to set the terms of civic participation and to define the standards by which the execution of those terms would be judged.

The Boss

When I accepted a counseling position at Harvard Business School, I knew that my skills would be tested frequently by the academically gifted and competitive students who would be my clients. I was also aware that for all of their successes and comfort with intellectual challenges, they would find it more difficult to bear the vulnerability that personal growth typically entails.

That insight, however, did little to prepare me for Ken. Wearing a starched white buttoned-down shirt and "mirror-polished" shoes, Ken strode into my office and positioned his 6'3" frame in a chair directly opposite me. He folded his arms across his chest and before I could utter a word asked: "So what can I do for you?" (If you find yourself momentarily confused by this greeting, so was I.) As in most school mental health centers the client and the therapist were assigned; they did not get to choose each other.

Guessing that anxiety might have been the source of this unusual greeting, I responded by saying, "Why don't we start by your telling me what brought you in today?"

Given that opening, Ken said: "Well, I can tell you this right now. I'm a White, conservative, male Republican. I'm not one of you people who believe that other people should solve your problems." We will return to my relationship with Ken in later chapters. Suffice it now to say in spite of this inauspicious beginning, we went on to form a caring and productive relationship that lasted throughout his time in graduate school.

I describe Ken as "The Boss" because he chose to keep me at bay by asserting his "better than" position in the racial hierarchy. Finding himself in a vulnerable position with someone whom he considered to be "less than," he initially attempted to reverse roles by inquiring about my needs (i.e., "So what can I do for you?"). That tactic failed to establish his dominance when he was reminded that it was he who had come into my office with a particular need. At that point, with his defenses raised even higher, he became full-on insulting.

Although Ken had not chosen me as his therapist, he was not obliged to accept the assignment. Upon seeing a brown-skinned, female therapist whose competence he could not accept, he could have requested another counselor. He also had the option to walk out of the appointment at any time. I call his interaction with me a strategy of disconnection because Ken clearly wanted to hang on to the relationship; he just needed to have unilateral control of the terms of engagement.

As shown in these scenarios, internalized dominance and the derivative strategies of disconnection are not always born of ill intention. However, they always function to corroborate particular relational images about the roles and expectations associated with racial group membership. This function, which is not inconsequential, manifests in a variety of ways, from the merely insulting to the lethal.

Merely insulting might be the punchline in a joke about "the smartest black man in the world" jumping to his death because he thought a backpack was a parachute. Or it might be the notion, expressed by one former U.S. president that members of Native American tribes should feel *honored* to see caricatures of themselves emblazoned on sports jerseys (Associated Press, 1991). Lethal would be the criminalization of the presence of a member of the dominated or "less than" group, as in the arrest of a Black male gardening in a vacant lot, or the killing of an unarmed Black teenager who was presumed not to belong in a certain neighborhood.

The point is this: One group—the dominant group—feels entitled to determine how the dominated group will be known and portrayed, in which spaces they can exist and on what terms. These portrayals then reify existing relational images, thus serving to further justify how members of the dominated "less than" group may participate in the social order. The Missionary, The Presumptive Judge, and The Boss are admittedly broad-brush portraits. They are not intended to capture the full complexity of these cross-racial interactions. They are variations on the theme of internalized dominance. Although this belief system may or may not be part of conscious awareness, it is an identity lens through which responses to questions about purpose, place, and possibility are developed and enacted.

INTERNALIZED OPPRESSION

Internalized oppression is a social–political construct that has gained wide familiarity over the years. In general terms, it manifests in the cognitive-emotional and behavioral patterns of a person who enacts or otherwise colludes with negative stereotypes about her own social identity group (e.g., race, ethnicity, class, sexual orientation). With specific reference to internalized racism, Donna Bivens (1995) has advanced the understanding of this relational dynamic with clarity and precision.

According to Bivens, internalized racism cannot be conflated with other realities such as low self-esteem, colorism, stereotyping, and self-hatred. Rather, she views internalized racism as a systemic oppression that has a life of its own, resulting in structural disadvantage that undermines politically the power of people and communities of color. It is not simply a personal problem.

Because race is a political construct that comes out of histories of domination and exploitation, the internalization of negative beliefs impacts people of color cross-culturally as well as intra-culturally. For example, people of color may be pitted against each other to secure proximity to the White norm. My daughter Angela sometimes refers to this divisiveness as the "Pick Me Pathology." Like internalized dominance, internalized oppression manifests in strategies of disconnection that aim at unilateral control of relationships. Although they may provide apparent and temporary advantage, they ultimately result in a diminution of relational integrity and possibility.

For the purpose of illustration, I will provide three scenarios—The Mascot, The Race Eraser, and The Chosen One—to illustrate how these strategies might operate in racialized contexts.

The Mascot

The strategy of the Mascot is important because it defies intuition. She or he may have less structural power in the relationship, but that reality does little to contravene the person's efforts to exert nearly unilateral control over the relationship. In work settings, the "Mascot" may appear to be no more consequential than a good-natured bumbler; but make no mistake, he is typically much more clear-eyed about his relational tactics and goals than his supervisors might ever suspect.

Take for example the case of Floyd, an African American social studies teacher in a predominantly White magnet school. Floyd was not at all happy about his assignment to the school. For the better part of his 20-year career, Floyd had worked in a school close to the neighborhood where he grew up. When the school was closed due to system budget cuts, the choice was early retirement or reassignment. The choice was not easy for school administrators either, given that in his old school Floyd was known as a beloved "character," but not an especially strong performer.

With the transfer, Floyd became a social studies teacher by default. The same budget cuts that caused the school closure also eliminated the vocational education department in which Floyd taught for most of his 20 years. Reluctant to lay off such a likeable and, in many ways, multifunctional employee, his new principal inserted him into the social studies department, where it was presumed he would work to retirement.

Knowing that he couldn't demonstrate the level of content proficiency valued by his colleagues, Floyd found a way to make himself likeable, thereby securing his niche in his new professional community. Also, since some community members were calling for a more multicultural curriculum, Floyd was assigned to teach Black history, a course for which there was no standard syllabus. Feeling that he had already "done his time," Floyd had no interest in enrolling in professional development coursework that might have helped him to feel more competent in his new role.

Instead, he compensated by staying "just a few pages ahead" of his students, making extensive use of movies in the classroom, regaling them with jokes, and, much to their delight, occasionally showing up with sugar cookies and cupcakes straight from his oven. In addition, Floyd could always be counted on to chaperone bus trips, contribute to bake sales, or perform in fund-raising talent shows. He was first to show up at pep rallies, wearing the mascot gear, collecting tickets for sports and extracurricular events.

It's not that Floyd was deluded about his performance or his colleagues' appraisal of his capabilities. He simply knew that his qualifications for the job would go unchallenged so long as he distracted his supervisors with his likeability and usability. What his supervisors saw was good-natured, smiling, but "not-quite-qualified" Floyd, someone they tolerated in order not to make waves and someone who contributed to the face of diversity in the school. Knowing that he had neither the aspiration nor the acuity to take on the challenging students, they allowed him to serve out his tenure teaching a course with little oversight or credibility in the department.

This arrangement allowed the administrators to hold on to their relational images of themselves (e.g., tolerant of diversity) while not fully respecting their colleague and calling him to professional accountability. Unknown to them, Floyd intentionally used likeability and humor to outsmart and distract. His strategy of disconnection compromised not only the potential of his students, but the dignity that he felt was his due.

When I first met Floyd and learned how he was navigating his preretirement years, I was reminded of a conversation I had with a young Afro-Caribbean undergraduate. She described her experience in her first racially integrated school in this way. "I know exactly how to get what I want from White people. They like it when I smile at them. So I do. Then I put out my hand and get what I want and leave them. They never know the difference."

The Race Eraser

Jeannette was stunned when a Latinx nursing student asked her why she disliked the Black students so much. To Jeannette, a nursing supervisor in a large teaching hospital, the critique was not only impertinent and hurtful, it was just plain wrong. She wanted all of the young nurses whom she managed to be successful, and none more than the Black students, whose abilities she feared might be questioned in the environment. She was also intent on showing the members of her medical team that she would hold all students in her charge strictly accountable for quality performance; she did not want to be seen showing "racial favoritism."

She did, however, acknowledge her frustration with the students who insisted on bringing their "ghetto ways" to the classroom and onto the nursing floor. In her view, ghetto ways consisted of everything from their conversational style to music choices to their ethnically conspicuous hair designs. "Why," she demanded of one student, "would she waste so much time watching the televised funeral of [legendary singer] Aretha Franklin?" She went on to say to a White colleague that Miss Franklin "did not represent her culture!"

Knowing something of Jeannette's family background was helpful in understanding how she chose to navigate her work environment. Jeannette had grown up in the coastal South, the only child of a schoolteacher and a postal worker. Her parents spared no effort to ensure that she would be able to succeed in the changing cultural environment of the 1970s, when, among other changes, schools were becoming racially integrated. Her parents' job was to work hard to afford the violin and piano lessons and exposure to "high culture."

Jeannette's job was to demonstrate excellence, and thereby dispel any doubt that she belonged in these previously segregated arenas. For all of her hard work, however, she was not immune to casual insults, including those that attributed the presence of Black people in college classrooms to affirmative action legislation. Her reaction to these slights was to double down on proving she belonged—even if some other Black people didn't. In fact, while in college she made a point of distancing herself from activities that were seen as stereotypically Black. She insisted on broadcasting the fact that she grew up listening to opera, not rhythm and blues. Upon graduation from college, she continued to distinguish herself by dint of hard work and by distancing herself from any association that might cause her to be seen as a member of a "less than" group.

It wasn't that she was unaware or unbothered by racial biases; she was actually hyperaware of the biases that occasionally inflected performance appraisals. As a nursing supervisor and member of the hospital quality assurance team, she was sometimes privy to what she thought were racially disparaging remarks about a young student or doctor. However, she also feared that to speak up in their defense would be to diminish her professional credibility. Jeannette had grown up during an era when it was important to be a "credit to her race." Individual excellence was a path toward racial uplift.

The problem was that excellence was defined as approximating dominant cultural norms. When her young student accused her of disliking Black people, the remark carried a bitter sting. The irony of her situation was that she attempted to gain respect by *disconnecting* from the vitality and fullness of her own experience, showing only the parts of herself that she thought would earn approval and acceptance from White people. In other words, to be a credit to her race, she attempted to erase her race.

The Chosen One

After working 7 years in a large advertising firm, David had finally secured his position in the middle echelons of management. He enjoyed the cachet of being associated with a high profile company and aspired to ever-higher levels of responsibility. Being designated as a manager-mentor of a new employee was an indicator of his upward trajectory in the company. He enjoyed working with Manuel, a newly minted MBA who like himself identified as Dominican.

His new mentee was a quick study, gaining credibility with clients and respect from other associates in the firm. Within just a few months, Manuel was getting assigned to high-profile projects while learning from the experience that David had gained over the years. David, however, learned that he had a problem. His supervisor, Vanessa, also Latinx, experienced Manuel as a "bit too cocksure" of himself. She had worked her way up the ladder over several years and felt uncomfortable with Manuel's easy camaraderie with senior executives. She began commenting on Manuel's penchant for "social climbing," insinuating that his ascent in the company would jeopardize David's opportunities for future promotion. She pointed out that Manuel was getting invited to meetings that even she, as David's supervisor, had never attended. The *sub voce* warning was that Manuel was a threat to their careers. Vanessa reminded David of what she called "the politics of diversity": There was not room at the top for all of them. For his part, Manuel started to notice that David seemed to have less time for him, even though he had stepped in and brought a project to successful completion while David was out on an extended leave due to illness. The sidelining continued when David returned to work. Manuel found himself shifted to low-visibility community relations work.

What had started as a mutually respectful and supportive relationship between the two men eventually devolved into one characterized by a low-grade tension. Manuel was not surprised when he learned that David had reported to senior managers that he was uncertain of Manuel's fit and of his loyalty to the firm. Manuel left the firm after 2 years, but not before having a heart-to-heart conversation with David, who acknowledged that being the Chosen One was his pathway to success: that he had torpedoed Manuel's career in hopes of advancing his own.

STRATEGIES OF DISCONNECTION AND ILLUSIONS OF POWER-OVER

The strategies of disconnection described in the preceding scenarios are by no means exhaustive, neither in degree of intensity, nor complexity, nor kind. Moreover, it might be helpful to think of them as representing a continuum of enactments. For example, the Race Eraser may resort to strategies of disconnection that range from distancing (i.e., not wanting to be seen as one of "them") to active derogation (disparaging or otherwise seeking to harm "them"). Furthermore, the same strategy (e.g., erasure) may be enacted from either side of the power-over differential. From the standpoint of internalized dominance, the Race Eraser may be someone who professes not to see color at all—ever.

Additionally, overgeneralization is a strategy of disconnection that may operate from either belief system. From either standpoint, one "negative" behavior is generalized as wholesale proof of the inferiority or the malevolence of an entire racial group.

At the root of all strategies of disconnection is racialized anxiety about power, vulnerability, and scarcity. Beatrice Bruteau (2005) described this dynamic as the psychology of inequality. In Bruteau's analyses, the belief systems that I call internalized dominance and internalized oppression are actually interpolating dynamics: The dominator seeks to expand his or her sense of being by controlling the lives of others, defining himself in contrast to others, and using others as extensions of themselves. Likewise, the subject of domination may seek to enhance his or her sense of safety or status by behaving in ways that maintain the paradigm of inequality.

For example, the Missionary may need a Mascot in order for the dynamic to persist, and a Mascot is not effective without a willing Missionary. It is easy to see how these dynamics may be collusive.

Yet to assert that power-over strategies of disconnection may be enacted from either side of the differential is not to say that the actors have equal power. In fact, on the dominant or superior side of the differential, the actors may have sufficient structural or cultural power to force their targets to enact inferiority. They may do so by limiting any number of citizenship rights or by denying access to resources that enable a life of dignity. Under these circumstances, strategies of disconnection become necessary strategies of resistance. Put plainly, although one may be forced to *behave* as if she is inferior, she may not *believe* she is inferior. Under these circumstances, the disconnection between the adopted behaviors and internalized beliefs can be acts of resistance that preserve a sense of integrity and possibility.

In a culture of racial stratification, the dominating or "better than" group at the top of the hierarchy is not made more secure by their higher social status. In fact, their susceptibility to anxiety is heightened by the instability of power-over arrangements, in part because their hold on a superior status may seem quite fragile. They may seek to secure that status by derogating others; that is, reassuring themselves of superior entitlements by ascribing faults and failures to the dominated group. People in lower ranks who defy this perspective are regarded as presumptuous, arrogant, impudent, or "uppity" should they show more confidence than is appropriate for their lower status (Bruteau, 2005, p. 40).

The dominated or "less than" racial group may seek to allay anxiety by using strategies of disconnection that stabilize rather than deconstruct inequality. They may collude by committing exorbitant energy to managing how they are perceived by the "better than" group, or they may seek to gain security by ingesting the values, behaviors, and perspectives of the "better than" group. On the other hand, they may wrest control of the inequality by taking over the role of the dominator or "better than" group.

Finally, it must be re-emphasized that strategies of disconnection are attempts to survive in a culture of racial stratification. They aim to mitigate the chronic anxiety and endemic suffering caused by deep-structured in-equality. Furthermore, the behaviors associated with these strategies are not always inherently dysfunctional and may in some instances have short-term adaptive value. Context and intent are nuanced, critical considerations. What makes these strategies dysfunctional are three criteria:

1. They represent fear of *being* in relationship. Instead of fostering flow and emergent experience in relationship, they aim for unilateral or dominant control of relationship.
2. They reproduce a closed system, thereby locking the power differential in place.
3. They function to extract value *from* relationship, rather than to create value and new possibilities *in* relationship.

REFLECTIONS

Choose a trusted partner to discuss a time when you attempted to gain con-trol of a relationship by deploying strategies of disconnection, both from a standpoint of more power and less power. What were some of the fears/anx-ieties that may have motivated your behaviors? What were the outcomes—near term and long term? How would you describe the quality of trust in the relationship?

CHAPTER 5

Sticks and Stones and Words That Hurt

"If anyone in here can moonwalk, I know it's you!"

—comment made to the only African American attendee
at a 40th high school reunion

We've all heard, and perhaps said, the childhood ditty: "Sticks and stones may break my bones, but words will never hurt me." However, its message turns out to be patently untrue. Words hurt. Most of us readily recognize the "sticks and stones" of racism: It looks ugly, sounds repugnant, and can turn violent and lethal in a heartbeat. The aims of this kind of racism are clearly meant to establish and perpetuate disparate structures of access and opportunity. Equally important, such "sticks and stones racism" aims to inculcate a psychology of inequality in both the dominators and dominated.

But what about less easily interpreted words and behaviors, acts of omission and commission that depend for their meaning on race-based narratives about human purpose and possibility? These ambiguous encounters are filled with ambivalence and could quite possibly be explained away as normal. As noted in Chapter 2, Kovel (1970), in his book *White Racism: A Psychohistory*, referred to these actions as aversive racism. Other writers attribute the ambiguity to a conflict between negative feelings about Blacks and belief in an "egalitarian value system," both of which are derived from a racially stratified society (Gaertner & Dovidio, 1986, p. 62). Such a conflict holds two viewpoints to be true: Everyone is created equal, except that Blacks are less equal than Whites.

AVERSIVE RACISM

Aversive racism does not show up in white, hooded sheets, nor does it come with burning crosses and tattooed swastikas. It may be conveyed by tone of voice, words spoken or not spoken, or averted eyes that signal lack of recognition. When the racial images that we hold of ourselves and others are shaped by the biases of the dominant culture, our encounters are bound to be fraught with anxiety, ambivalence, or perhaps avoidance. While the look and feel of aversive racism can be difficult to articulate, the consequences are deeply felt. Tanya's experience at a car dealership illustrates this point.

Having emigrated from Trinidad as a young teenager, Tanya often dreamed of what it meant to be successful in America. She went to cosmetology school and worked hard at her craft, eventually acquiring enough capital to purchase a home and her own salon. She couldn't have been prouder on the morning when she set out to purchase a luxury car, the final symbol of her professional success. Dressed in stylish clothes, she walked onto the showroom floor of a dealership that sold only high-end European imports. She looked at cars, opening the doors and inspecting the interiors for about 10 minutes, but no salesperson approached her. Thinking that perhaps she was feeling "overly sensitive," and desperately wanting to buy a car that day, she made several passes in front of the sales staff, trying to invite their attention. No one came forward to greet her. Some remained seated at desks presumably doing paperwork; others were drinking coffee and chatting in small groups. After about a half hour, she gave up and left the dealership in tears.

What was happening here? We might begin by acknowledging that being ignored by sales staff in a car dealership, where the norm is to sell aggressively, would be experienced as an anomaly by any of us. We would be puzzled, if not outright irritated. Without the overlay of a cross-racial context, we might even march up to one of the staff and demand attention! Now imagine how Tanya might have felt when the dealership staff, whom she described as consisting of several White men and one White woman, ignored her. Her ability to purchase this high-end import meant more than mere transportation to Tanya. It was material proof of her standing: evidence that with her hard work she had "made it" and that she belonged to the ranks of high-achievers in our American society. In fact, her careful attention to appearance before entering the dealership was an attempt to ward off any suspicion that she did not belong. (*By the way, this kind of surface adornment is not uncommon among people who have learned to anticipate disrespect.*) Her best efforts, however, did nothing to help her gain the recognition and respect that she sought. It did not signal to the people who ignored her that she might actually have money! No one said a word to Tanya, but the aversive racism embedded in the silence was loud and clear: "You do not belong here. We do not see you."

Social Pain Overlap Theory

Tanya's tears expressed the social pain of exclusion. She left the dealership feeling diminished. The assault on her sense of self-worth was as real to her brain as a punch in the stomach. This experience can be seen through the lens of Social Pain Overlap Theory, or SPOT. Through experiments in their UCLA laboratory, researchers Naomi Eisenberger, Matthew Lieberman, and Kipling Williams discovered that the pain of social exclusion is real (2003). Specifically, they found that under conditions of relatively mild social pain, the part of the brain that is responsible for picking up signals of physical pain (i.e., dorsal anterior cingulate cortex—dACC) is activated. They further discovered that the more the social-emotional pain intensified, the more activated the dACC became.

Why does any of this matter? It matters because our brains have evolved to yearn for belonging and connection. It matters because we thrive when we are in mutually rewarding relationships. Psychiatrist Amy Banks offers a brilliant analysis of the workings of our evolutionarily complex mammalian brains. In their book *Four Ways to Click: Rewire Your Brain for Stronger, More Rewarding Relationships*, Banks and Hirschman (2015) provided a memorable explanation of the distinction between our reptile brain or "reptilian independence" and our human brain that has evolved to thrive in connection:

- Reptiles don't have the neural equipment that causes them to feel pain when they are left out of a social group.
- Reptiles don't possess a nerve that uses welcoming facial signals to modulate stress.
- Reptiles don't need to know that other reptiles "get them."

Like the rest of us, Tanya was obviously not a lizard, but an adult human with a personal (i.e., relational-cultural) history that shaped her self-image, hence her needs, longings, and expectations. She got none of what she needed from her encounter with the sales staff. She left that encounter with the experience of "less than" being more deeply imprinted in her brain.

In Tanya's case no words were spoken, but to my client Glenda the social pain was caused by words.

What's So Funny about Aunt Jemima?

Having lived in a small New England town all of her life, Glenda was not surprised when she was the only or one of a few Black people in any setting. And so it was when she enrolled in an adult education class to learn Spanish; she was the only person of African descent in a class of about 25 adults. The class was taught by a young woman who identified as Puerto Rican. The instructor was very likeable; her energy and her jokes kept the nighttime class of work-weary adults moving along at a lively pace.

One night, the instructor told a story about being lost in a Detroit airport. There was nobody around that she could talk to, and the only person who helped her was a woman who looked like *"that lady . . . you know*

. . . I don't know her name but she's big (with hand gestures) dark-skinned, big smile, and she's on that pancake box!" Someone in the class helped by saying, *"Oh you mean Aunt Jemima,"* to which the instructor exclaimed *"Yes, that one!"* The teacher and the rest of the class then laughed together at the amusing incident.

Glenda didn't laugh. She didn't say a word because she couldn't think of a word to say, or more precisely, any that would have served her well. At the end of the session that night, she left and never returned.

When Glenda and I spoke nearly a week later, she was still visibly stung by the experience. She knew she felt angry; in fact her anger at her instructor increased each time she recounted the incident to other friends and family members. (Quite likely, in the retelling she used some of the words she could not use in class that night.) However, she couldn't decide where the anger should land and in what proportion. *Did the conversation happen because of the casual bigotry of her classmates? Was the instructor just culturally oblivious?* She also felt humiliated. Her classmates and the instructor were in on a joke that did not include her. Except that it did. She felt that she *was* the joke.

The confusion and self-doubt came later in our conversation. *Was she being overly sensitive? Was it really such a big deal?* As Miller (1988) pointed out in her working paper *Connections, Disconnections and Violations,* this reaction is fairly typical. In the face of a violation of any sort, the target of the violation may first disconnect and invalidate her own experience.

As we talked it through, Glenda began to realize her susceptibility to shaming by stereotype. In this case it was "Mammy," represented in the cultural imagination (and hence on commercial products) as a large-sized, brown- or black-skinned woman whose only life purpose is to provide aid and comfort to White people. Mammy functions as a cultural trope in popular literature from *Gone with the Wind* to *The Help.* Her lovability is dependent entirely upon her willing servility; she knows and relishes her "less than" place in the racial hierarchy. She is fiercely protective and devoted to her White masters, but not especially smart.

While Glenda recognized that her real life bore no resemblance to the fictional Jemima, she also knew that stereotypes obliterate distinctions. They not only justify existing power relations among groups in a racialized society, they titrate the gradations of respect to which any individual member of a group might be entitled. *What if she too were seen as a serviceable, but laughable, character? Did her teacher's and her classmates' laughter signal their affirmation of the stereotype? How did their affirmation of the stereotype color the relational lens through which they viewed her?*

Not surprisingly, Glenda was ashamed of feeling ashamed. She wondered if her embarrassment stemmed from a wish to distance herself from earlier generations of Black women, many of whom had few options other than domestic service to support their families. Our conversation extended over a period of weeks, and at one point, I decided it was appropriate to share the following personal experience with her.

A few months earlier, my husband and I attended a party celebrating his 40th high school reunion. In a room of almost 300 people, I was the only African American. When the DJ started playing a string of Michael Jackson tunes, a woman whom I did not know smiled at me and said: "Well if anyone in here can moonwalk, I know it's you!" (It was a *40th* reunion; the room was filled with creaky knees, and I quite frankly would have been surprised if anyone could moonwalk!)

In my heart of hearts, I knew that the woman at the reunion was making a friendly gesture; her comment was meant as a compliment. Yet, I was miffed. I explained to Glenda that I eventually realized that my irritation was a thin cover for a deeply felt sense of helplessness—namely, my inability to fend off stereotypic expectations. The woman did no more than what any of us might do on any given day. She took one piece of information (i.e., my skin color) and extrapolated a narrative about me, thereby revealing her relational images (I'm guessing) about middle-aged Black women.

Were it not for the racialized context, I might have responded in a more polite manner, rather than with a curt "I don't think so." There are many ways I might have responded in that awkward moment: maybe something as simple as introducing myself and asking her name. I might have inquired if she were a member of the reunion class or a guest like me. Instead, my internalized narratives got activated. If she could have read the thought bubbles above my head, she would have seen something like this:

- "White people expect Black people to sing and dance."
- "I am not here to provide entertainment for them."

Although I can't moonwalk, I love to dance. However, on that night my reaction was very similar to my client Glenda's. I had no desire to dance. I can only imagine that I wasn't the only person who walked away from that brief encounter feeling a little "off." *What happened between us was a classic model of disconnection. Instead of encountering each other as persons, we both led with our internalized relational images.*

Relational Images

No doubt relational images can be helpful as we try to navigate social spaces filled with uncertainties and the unknown. For example, when we approach any encounter, it is completely useful and appropriate to bring expectations based on our histories and our repertoire of cultural knowledge. It's as simple as this: When I walk into the dentist's office, I expect to have my teeth examined—not my feet. I expect to pay for the dentist's services. Such base-level expectations are part of being a functioning member in that cultural space. However, when we go much beyond that base level, extrapolating meaning and imputing intent, is when we miss the openings and new possibilities that may emerge in a relationship. We start to create thin stories of reality that conform to the contours of our pre-made images.

Our internalized, pre-made images—that all Black people are as expert a moonwalker as Michael Jackson or as unfailingly helpful as Aunt Jemima—help us make our relationship stories simpler and seemingly more navigable. However, as theologian and scholar Karen King argues, we are better served by stories with loose ends, multiple voices, and contradictions. In other words, we need complex stories for the complexity of our lives (Gibson, 2018). Ultimately, our internalized images do not serve us well. As psychologist and RCT scholar Irene Stiver explained, when we respond to an image with an image, we are moving away from relationship and toward an impasse (Miller & Stiver, 1995).

Words hurt, particularly when expressed as stereotypes that strip away the right to name the variability and fluidity of one's own experience. (Remember, with "power-over" or "better than" positioning comes the entitlement to define the terms—i.e., place, purpose, possibilities—of the "less than" group.) As a function of both historical and contemporary racial stratification, idiosyncratic distinctions among members of the "less than" group are rendered irrelevant. It is the voice of the "better than" group saying, "You are who I say you are."

LANGUAGE AS CODIFIED RACISM

Social pain is by definition a relational experience that reverberates beyond any specific or single interpersonal encounter. Words that reflect, produce, and validate disconnection engender strife and suffering that pervade the culture. Because one pillar of 21st-century American idealism is equality of opportunity, such phrases are typically part of a coded language that has one purpose: to codify racism. Commonly known as "dog whistles," such language constructs fear-based narratives that justify separation, whether through constricted access to resources or outright exclusion from opportunity. What's tricky is that the words themselves may sound plausible, even noble.

Take for example the phrase, "religious freedom," which sounds like a right of American citizenship. However, this phrase has been used to pit one group of citizens against another by codifying discrimination based on sexual orientation, as when those whose religious beliefs include only heterosexuality cite their right to religious freedom as a rationale to discriminate against people who are LGBTQ+. "Immigrant caravan" is more than a colorful phrase. When used to evoke anti-immigrant emotions, the phrase conjures up images of dark-skinned hordes threatening to invade American borders. Here's another example. In Massachusetts, a 2012 state election campaign featured a robocall in which one candidate promised to protect "suburban residents" from economic exploitation caused by "urban" residents. In the cultural imagination, "urban" has become a code word for Black or Brown (depending on one's geography) whether in reference to music or violence. The notion of boundary threat—whether from immigrant caravans or urban residents—is a powerful inducement to protective divisiveness, creating invisible fault lines throughout the culture. These fault lines normalize the interpersonal wariness and antipathy that underscore racism.

FALSE NARRATIVES

Although everyone suffers from the disconnection, suffering may manifest differently depending upon one's location in the racialized hierarchy. Although people of color are the more visible victims of institutional discrimination and violence in education, law enforcement, health care and so forth, the culture of White supremacy exacts a cost from White people as well. Being White and male places an American human at the top of two social hierarchies, both of which also represent the greatest risk of death by suicide (O'Brien, 2018). The Jungian philosopher James Hillman (1964) attributes this phenomenon to the internalization of extreme individualism, or what I call the *Separate Self Imperative*. Although it is a highly valorized myth in American culture, the Separate Self Imperative breeds fear and shame. It is the notion that predicates social rank on rugged individualism and control. Therefore, any demonstration of need or loss of control is deemed evidence of unworthiness in a racially stratified culture. Moreover, this fear and shame may account in part for the rage-filled violence evidenced by the spate of racially motivated killings of the past decade (Eligon, 2018).

Paul Kivel (1997) suggests that the anxiety and rage endemic to notions of White supremacy starts with the inculcation of false narratives. One such narrative is that the early "American" colonizers discovered a vast wilderness, befriended and exchanged presents with the native populations, and through their industry, perseverance, and godliness created a noble civilization. The resulting American identity narrative is filled with ellipses that deny or reframe the violence, exploitation, and international human trafficking through which the colonizers accomplished their goals.

To maintain such a narrative one must be ever vigilant in constructing and fortifying the protective boundaries that hold the identity illusion, the "better than" position in the hierarchy of human worth. For all of their apparent grandiosity, supremacist identities are fraught with status anxiety. Remember in Chapter 4 my story of "The Boss," Ken, who attempted at the outset of the relationship to establish his dominance over me, his African

American counselor? His impulse to disconnect was based not so much on personal animosity (he didn't know me) but on his anxiety about his need or responsibility to protect the boundaries of racial superiority. In other words, if he could not be "better than," he ran the risk of feeling worthless. A quote attributed to Indian philosopher Jiddu Krishnamurti aptly describes Ken's dilemma: He thought he was thinking his own thoughts, but he was thinking the culture's thoughts (Fonda, 2016).

We are not always aware when we are thinking the culture's thoughts, precisely because these thoughts seem so normal. Often only under conditions of disequilibrium, such as a difficult encounter, do these thoughts rise to the level of consciousness. A culture of chronic and pervasive disconnection deconstructs our capacities for cultivating the trust and mutual respect required for growth and authentic being. When the culture itself is the agent of disconnection, each of us is vulnerable to getting trapped inside a small story of who we are and who we can become, a limited imagination of human possibility.

21ST-CENTURY LINGUISTIC DILEMMAS: THE "N" WORD

Just before I was scheduled to give a conference keynote, I took a seat at a table with a mixed-race group of young college women. One of them, an African American whom I will call Tamara, turned to me and said: "I googled you and read that you moved to New England as an adult. What was it like moving to a new culture?"

I had no idea how to answer her, because frankly, I didn't know what she was asking. I mumbled something about differences in social styles, but our conversation was cut short because it was time for me to give my talk. Her question stayed with me because I knew I hadn't answered whatever she was asking. When I saw her a few days later, I told her that I had enjoyed meeting her and felt that our conversation got cut short. With that invitation, she explained to me that she had grown up in North Carolina in a very diverse community where people knew how to get along. Her college, however, was in a small conservative town in Virginia. To help her mother cover the costs, she took a part-time job in a large supermarket. She said to me: "Within the first week I was there, I had been called nigger twice." The store manager minimized the incident by saying "that's just how these old people are around here." Her mother had admonished her to keep her temper so that she could keep her job.

Her hurt was palpable, and I could feel the pain vibrating in the space between us. Her hurt was due not only to the insult but to the dismissal of the insult. She was given two options: Don't feel the pain, or if you must feel it, don't do anything about it. Of course those options didn't work for Tamara because, as she put it: "I'm the kind of person who tells people exactly what I think!" That wasn't exactly true either; the gap between her idealized self and her lived reality created another overlay of pain and shame. Without trusting connections with others, Tamara was left isolated with a festering pain.

I felt deeply for her, and I wished I had some pithy retort for her to use whenever she encountered the situation again—as I knew she surely would. We needed more time than the few minutes our schedules allowed, but after a few moments of shared outrage, we were able to move rather quickly into a conversation about fully feeling, a process best approached in the presence of a trusted other. Tamara very much wanted to be "strong," and in trying to enact that image, she often conflated courage with bravado. Fortunately, she got it that she was best able to respond to painful encounters when she could ground herself in accepting her own feelings—even when acceptance included feeling dumbstruck.

The inherent toxicity of the word has been such that we call it the "n-word," unspeakable except in the mouths of avowed racists. Yet I was struck by the 21st-century linguistic dilemma that not only Tamara's generation, but all of us, must navigate. My brief conversation with Tamara left me thinking more seriously about four questions: (1) who can say the word "nigger"; (2) under what circumstances; (3) for what purpose; and (4) with what effect.

The n-word is now standard vocabulary in the hip-hop glossary. Likewise, a number of Black cultural provocateurs make liberal use of the word—sometimes (*I* believe) for shock value, sometimes as a dare, and sometimes as an act of resistance. The truth is also that in the past, the "n-word" was a part of "in-house" humor. Now, in the age of social media and global transmission of cultural norms and mores, there is no "in-house" humor that can be claimed as the exclusive provenance of any one group.

Of course, this issue predates the Internet age. Back in the late 1970s I sat next to one of my White students at a high school basketball game. His father was the owner of a radio station that played rhythm and blues, or "Black" music. At one point he looked at me and made a casual reference to "niggers." And then, as if on a dare, he said, "If they can call each other niggers, why can't I?" Like Tamara, I didn't have a pithy retort for that young man. I too had a job to keep, so unadulterated fury was not an option. Instead, I had to satisfy my outrage by asking him if there were other ways that he wanted to be like Black people. (It was a purely rhetorical question: I was not really interested in his answer.)

These are questions that will not go away; in fact, they seem to have become more pressing and deserve our careful consideration. For help with the questions, I decided to turn to teenagers, young adults (under 35), and a couple of in-house pundits of my own to get their perspectives on words that hurt. When is the n-word hurtful? To whom is it hurtful, and what makes it so? I also asked: If "nigger" is used as a reference for Black people, is there a similar reference for White people?

On occasion, I have asked the questions of a few young people of different racial-ethnic backgrounds, typically between the ages of 17 and 30. The responses I received, while widely divergent, were thoughtful and nuanced. First, there was fairly unanimous agreement that the word "nigger" is singular in its longevity and severity as a demeaning racial term. Although they acknowledged the existence of words like "cracker" and the short-lived "honky," there was agreement to a person that these words never had the punch or the cultural heft of a word like "nigger." Interestingly, some of my conversation partners pointed out that the word "White" spoken by a Black person is offensive to some White people, presumably because it feels like an accusation. In these cases, it is as if White has become synonymous with the word racist.

The responses to Who can say the word "nigger," when, and why have been much more varied. Some respondents of varied ethnicity simply consider it "the third rail" of social relations. "Just don't go there," they said. Some Black respondents spoke about using the word "nigger" as an act of resistance: reclaiming a potent toxin and repurposing it as an antidote to the shame for which it was originally intended.

Still others talked about the use of the word as an in-your-face challenge to White people, citing the conflicts that arise when a White person dares to speak the word either in the lyrics of a song or in conversation. For example, when the singer Madonna posted an Instagram photograph of her son with the hashtag "disnigga," she created a firestorm of controversy and ill-will (Fisher, 2014). Comedian-cum-political-pundit Bill Maher sparked similar outrage when he referred to himself as a "house nigger" (Itzkoff, 2017).

Most of the respondents acknowledged that no matter who uses the word or for what purpose, there remains the undertone of degradation. With regard to music, one person worried that the addictive beats enter the bodies and brains of young people in ways that conceal embedded messages of self-hate and limited possibility. To the extent that this happens, young brains may deeply internalize belief systems that encode images of Blackness as deserving permanent status on the lower rungs of the racial hierarchy. Across generations and across racial groupings, our interdependencies are such that the toxicity of this internalization seeps through our cultural membranes contaminating our places of encounter. When that happens, words hurt.

REFLECTIONS

1. Have there been times when you "caught yourself" saying or doing something that runs counter to your values? How might that

experience reflect Krishnamurti's concept of "thinking the culture's thoughts"? Under what conditions has this happened and how did you respond?

2. Recall a time when you either experienced or witnessed an incident when someone did or did not say something that was potentially hurtful. What did you feel? What concerns did you have? Did you want to respond? Whether you did or did not, what was "at stake" for you?

CHAPTER 6

Disruptive Empathy

Beyond "I Feel Your Pain"

None of us is a discrete, separate unit, but an integrated system of
interactions and relationships connected to all.

—Judy Cannato

When I watched a film of the eminent psychologist Carl Rogers working
with his client "Gloria," (1965) all of my thoughts were variations on a
single theme: "How can I ever be this good?" I really wanted to be "*that
good.*" Here was a man of infinite patience and nearly clairvoyant wisdom.
He seemed the perfect embodiment of kindness, acceptance, and knowing
beyond his client's capacity to know. How could "Gloria" not heal and
flourish in the presence of his unconditional positive regard?

My understanding of empathy has evolved over the years, probably
as much out of moral necessity as professional maturity. Like my peers-in-
training, I tried mightily to emulate Rogers's stance. Our thinking was that
with enough positive regard and unconditional caring, no client's experience
would be so foreign and no pain so disabling as to undermine the efficacy of
our healing power. Empathy was the instrument we would wield to conquer
pain. We never spoke in such militaristic terms; however, we did compete in
what we later laughingly called the "Empathy Olympics." In group supervision settings, we would notice which of us could feel the pain of another
so deeply that she would shed a tear. No doubt we also silently scoffed at
anyone who seemed unfeeling or lacking in this numinous capacity. I now
think of this phase of training as a developmental rite of passage, one in
which we were all earnestly striving to prove ourselves worthy of our chosen
profession.

Without a doubt, further learning and professional maturity revealed the
limitations of this mindset. Under the careful and caring guidance of mentors and supervisors, we grew beyond notions of empathy as a performance.
And the lesson was clear: When we practice empathy as a performance of
"I feel your pain," we quickly run up against our human limitations. We
can—and in some professions we must—cultivate the capacity to apprehend
the emotions of another person. Whether in education or mental health
practice, accurate empathy or the dispositional attitude of the counselor

(Carkhuff, 2000) is essential to furthering growth, healing, and learning. However, to persist in the "empathy as performance" mindset quite predictably leads to two options: to dissemble and feel like an imposter, or to dissemble and rationalize the interaction as necessarily transactional—a mere means to a desired outcome.

If everyone agrees that empathy is a good thing, why is there so little of it evident in our 21st-century American life? Perhaps it is the performance mindset that largely accounts for what is commonly described as an empathy deficit, particularly noticeable in well-meaning cross-racial interactions. Given our peculiar histories and culturally patterned interactions, sometimes the chasm of difference is too wide and deep to be easily navigated. It is then that strategies of disconnection are likely to come into play: pretending to care and to connect by withholding or suppressing vital aspects of our experience—not only from the other person, but from ourselves.

DISRUPTIVE EMPATHY

There is another option, one that I have come to call disruptive empathy. Disruptive empathy is a process of engagement that facilitates movement toward a level of open-heartedness and open-mindedness that can take in all that appears to be "Utterly Other"—even when, or especially when, the "Otherness" appears in ourselves. Disruptive empathy helps us to remain mindful that what we experience as "Other" is a part of the humanity that we all share. This process is disruptive because it requires a certain level of willful destabilization. Specifically, we have to loosen our attachment to the narratives about self and other. We must be willing to be surprised and accepting of parts of ourselves we previously found embarrassing or shameful. That is no small feat given that our identity narratives, often painstakingly constructed, provide a schema for how the world works. In other words, they secure our sense of purpose and place; they guide our movement, insinuating "next steps" in any given interaction. Another distinguishing aspect of disruptive empathy is that it involves courage more than comfort. I make that distinction because conventional notions of empathy may evoke images of warmth, agreement, and harmony. Disruptive empathy, in contrast, may be the portal to conflict, the space where new possibilities might emerge.

Model Me and Not Me

We all carry around a Model Me identity of how we want to be seen in the world. Capable, smart, attractive, and yes, empathic are all qualities that most of us aspire to embody. In the racial identity narratives that we all construct, the Model Me is likely to be a fixed and idealized image.

The Not Me we all carry around is a cartoonish devil that sits on our shoulder making us say or do the things we might otherwise find distasteful. It's the voice that says or does things about which we're likely to feel embarrassed or ashamed. When the Not Me voice emerges—usually out of nowhere—is when we need to listen carefully.

To illustrate, here's a story about the healing possibilities that emerge when we can let go of our Model Me identity and listen to the Not Me voice. Haley, a young woman, came into my office more than a little irritated with her best friend, Kim. Haley was a mixed-race woman, the only daughter of an Irish mother and Trinidadian father. Most people, however, simply saw her as White, a "mistake" that both she and her best friend Kim found laughable. Kim identified as African American, and anyone who saw her would assume she was.

The conflict between the friends arose one day when they went shopping together. Twice while they were in the store, White women customers walked up to the two friends and asked Kim for assistance finding something. According to Haley, both she and Kim laughed off the first incident as a typical racial annoyance. Kim never knew when people would assume she was "the help." A few minutes later, a second White woman walked up to Kim and demanded that she go and find something for her. This time, it wasn't funny to Kim. She yelled at the woman: "What makes you think I work here?" The woman yelled back: "Well, thank you for your kindness, Miss!" At that point, Haley laughed and walked away. That was when she saw Kim glaring at her.

A little later, Haley tried to engage Kim in friendly chatter, but Kim was silent. When Haley eventually asked Kim if she was angry, Kim replied, "No. Hurt." She accused Haley of not being an ally when she most needed one. Haley explained that she was preoccupied with finals and "just didn't have time to deal with all that racial drama," but she did apologize to Kim for walking away. She was more than stung by Kim's response: "You get to use your light skin privilege to choose when you want to deal with racism. My skin is brown, and I don't get to choose when it's a good day to notice whether I'm being racially profiled."

Haley found Kim's response completely unwarranted and overblown. She was aware that although they continued to spend time together, a palpable tension remained, conversation was strained, and activities together less spontaneous.

What had happened between these two women who loved each other? The incidents in the store, unnerving for both, were not the source of the ongoing disconnection. The ongoing strain was caused by their different racial narratives, how they thought about themselves in the world.

Haley and I talked about why she recoiled immediately from the notion of "light skin privilege." Her response again was immediate: "Because I'm not that kind of person!" Haley's Model Me, an ally and best friend to Kim, sensitized to racial issues, daughter of mixed-race parentage, did not identify with light-skinned privilege. For Haley, light-skinned privilege was Not Me. I knew that she wanted to heal the breach with her friend, but I also knew that would be quite unlikely until she befriended her Not Me voice.

Over the course of two sessions, Haley was able to share what she liked about her light skin and silky curls, acknowledging that she enjoyed everyday conveniences that were denied her friend. Doing so didn't make her a bad person or any less "woke." In fact, bringing her Not Me into fuller voice made her more "woke." She went on to acknowledge that her laughter in response to the incidents came out of her anxiety and fear that she couldn't stand up to the woman who accosted her friend. Instead, she took refuge in what DiAngelo (2018) has termed White fragility.

Although a first response to a Not Me moment may be to recoil in anger or shame, a more helpful response is to regard it as a beckoning toward growth rather than deny its existence.

At the very least, the Not Me moments serve as a reminder that we do not live a single voice narrative. Model Me is where we feel safe. Not Me disrupts our preferred story about who we think we are.

In short, our narratives are comprised of multiple voices. Until we are willing to listen to (not necessarily agree with) all of the voices, we inhibit our movement into a more expansive experience of who we can be in the world. Disruptive empathy, in other words, begins at home.

Utterly Other

If Not Me stands as a counter-narrative to Model Me, there is another constellation of images that amplify the emotional weight of both. I call it Utterly Other. Utterly Other represents not only all that is Not Me, it signifies all that is absolutely repugnant, all that is regarded with suspicion and disdain. It is not difficult to conjure up such an image. Just think of some person—or some set of traits—that you consider to be outside the boundaries of human tolerance. Clearly the traits that mark the Utterly Other are those that we dare not see in ourselves. However, for that very reason, it might be helpful to regard Utterly Other as a potential breeding ground for our own "mind bugs," where disowned feeling-thoughts and biases fester out of conscious awareness.

THE ARC OF EMPATHY

We open the door to new possibilities through three transformative practices that I call the ARC of Empathy: Awareness, Respect, and Compassion. Conceptualizing empathy in these ways allows us to move beyond the traditional warm and fuzzy definitions. These more conventional notions of empathy may feel good, but they are ultimately difficult to practice and can be easily manufactured so as to become disingenuous. In contrast, practicing the ARC of empathy enlarges our capacity to cultivate more authentic relationships with one another.

The First Pillar in the ARC of Empathy: Awareness

We all laughed when my graduate school colleague recounted a conversation with her 9-year-old niece. It went like this.

> *Niece:* Auntie Lynn, I think I'm going to be a psychologist too.
> *Lynn:* Well that's very interesting. Why do you want to be a psychologist?
> *Niece:* Because you seem to like what you do, and it's easy. I already know how to do empathy. When someone tells you something, you just have to say "it feels like" or "sounds like" something. Or you can say, "I think I know what you feel."

As only a 9-year-old might do, Lynn's niece offered a pithy explanation of one of the core functions of empathy: to convey to another person that she has been heard. From a 9-year-old's point of view, nothing could be easier or more straightforward! Of course, the reality is that taking in and acknowledging the experience of another person is first and foremost an act of courage. It requires us to enter into that liminal space between knowing and not knowing, which not infrequently leads to disorienting ambiguity. Furthermore, taking in and acknowledging the experience of another can destabilize the narratives that are core to our sense of who we are in the world. This is the work of awareness.

As the first pillar of empathy, my shorthand definition of awareness is the revelatory process of signaling presence, commitment, and nonjudgmental witness. It is both internally and outwardly focused, enabling clear apprehension of the text, subtext, and context of an encounter.

Kids on Scooters. To illustrate this point, let me share a scenario that my client "Michael" discussed in our session one day. By way of context, Michael, a 20-something-year-old African American male, was a new homeowner in a rapidly gentrifying neighborhood. Less than a decade earlier, African Americans comprised almost 80% of the residents. With the influx of professional services and technology firms, roughly 60% of the residents currently described themselves as White. While scrolling through his social media feeds, Michael saw this alert on a neighborhood app. This is a snippet of the content.

Neighbor 1: One of our neighbors mentioned he saw kids on scooters
   looking into cars on Maple Street.
Neighbor 2: Call 911 for suspicious persons.
Michael: What does suspicious look like? Kids are curious, nosy, and
   clumsy by nature. Calling 911 is not a first action.
Neighbor 2: I was just advising. Do what you think is right and what
   you need. I thought that was what this post was. If I got it wrong
   or misunderstood it, I'm sorry.
Michael: I hear ya. I was advising too. Of course, 911 is a course
   for violence and emergencies, but as a new homeowner, I like to
   remember that these communities are older than my mortgage.
   I prefer to lead with "hello" rather than "what are you doing to
   me?"

You will notice that so far this exchange does not have the look and feel
of empathy. In fact, just the opposite: It looks and feels like neighbors on a
collision course toward conflict.

When I asked Michael to explain what triggered his decision to jump
into the online thread, he described a process of shifting between an internal
and external awareness. It began with taking notice of his own emotions
and the assumptions he was making about his neighbors. He assumed (*dare
I say like many of us who have now read this thread*) that the concerned
neighbors were White and the kids on scooters were Black. As an African
American male, he had had more than one potentially dangerous interaction
with police. Just a few months previous, he had been pulled over by police
on the flimsiest of pretexts. Shining flashlights in his face from both sides
of his vehicle, the officers questioned whether his headlights were working
properly before sending him on his way. The experience had been terrifying,
not only because it reflected the culturally acknowledged dangers of "driving while Black," but because it happened in a city where officers had twice
escaped penalties for killing unarmed Black males. Suffice it to say that the
immediate advice to call 911 triggered recall of that frightening experience.

Michael also knew that both he and his neighbors were building racialized narratives around sparse information, hence his opening question. Who
were the kids? How old were they? What did they look like? What were the
actual behaviors described as "looking in cars?" In addition to signaling his
presence and his point of view, Michael's decision to insert himself into the
conversation was an invitation to dialogue. It was not an effort to communicate simpatico feelings, nor was it an attempt to silence his neighbor. In
fact, he was saying, "tell me more."

Michael interpreted his neighbor's response to his question as "sorry,
not sorry." His deliberate use of a colloquialism, "I hear ya," was an attempt to forestall what he experienced as a defensive exit strategy, to soften

the tone of the exchange, and to facilitate more conversation. His empathic attunement to what his neighbor might have been feeling led him to use language that conveyed threat reduction. In other words, "I am not here to harm you." Let me say here that the thread did take many a wild and raucous turn among other neighbors who jumped into the fray, but the exchange between Michael and Neighbor 2 remained civil and respectful. These are the words that ended their exchange.

> *Neighbor 2:* I'm sorry this got blown way out of proportion, but the conversation has been helpful. I'm a White man living for the first time in a racially mixed neighborhood. I have good neighbors and I want to be a good neighbor. I need to remember that our different experiences and perspectives get in the way.
>
> *Michael:* Thanks. Every day is like a new moment of consciousness and focused intent.

The exchange between these two men who did not know each other exemplifies empathic awareness as explained by Judith Jordan in her 1984 paper, *Empathy and Self Boundaries*: a complex skill that involves joining with another in his or her emotional experience, while maintaining cognitive clarity. Jordan's definition demystifies empathy in that it captures both the dispositional stance and the operational practices that facilitate connection across difference.

Five Good Practices to Foster Awareness. In the spirit of what has become known as the Five Good Things of growth-fostering relationships, let me summarize this section with five good practices that foster awareness when confronting challenging racialized interactions.

1. Pause and breathe . . . open gently to your own experience: What am I thinking, feeling, remembering, desiring?
2. Become curious about yourself: Is some deep background story about yourself getting triggered?
3. Become curious about the other person: What are the stories and concerns behind the words being spoken?
4. Offer to engage in sharing differences; in other words, invite good conflict.
5. Open yourself to the possibility of seeing beyond the "first look" and of hearing beyond the first words. You will find yourself in that liminal space where new information emerges and disrupts old narratives. (Warning: the hardline boundaries between Self and Other may start to soften.)

The Second Pillar in the ARC of Empathy: Respect

Empathy is grounded in respect. Without respect, we end up with sympathy or sentimentality—neither of which makes room for the hard truths about the toxic disconnections endemic to a racially stratified culture. If our goal is to transform the meaning of race from a narrative of disconnection to one of connection, we can neither avoid nor assuage the toxic realities of our racialized histories. The chasm created by difference may simply be too vast, the racial violations too destructive to be ignored or sugarcoated away. Avoidance and assuagement are strategies of disconnection—ways of disengaging from the relationship. In other words, without the respect that enables truth telling, we undermine our human capacity for empathy.

Respect is an invitation to "otherness." It removes the constraints of sameness. Simply put, we don't have to identify with, agree with, or be attracted to another person in order to develop an empathic relationship. Respect signals curiosity, a tell-me-more stance that facilitates a loosening of the armor we carry to help us feel safe in racialized conflict. As the attitudinal stance of disruptive empathy, respect creates conditions that allow all participants in the relationship an opportunity to grow. Such was the case when I met "Pete" during the formative years of my training as a psychologist.

Disrobing: An Empathic Encounter with the KKK. When I met Pete, I was in my first official professional role as a group counselor on an inpatient addiction program. When he came onto the unit, he was already well known by the program staff and patients. His notoriety stemmed from his appearance on local television programs in his title as an exalted leader with the local Ku Klux Klan. While he could not literally wear his hood and robe on the hospital unit, they were nonetheless figuratively visible to me, his new-to-the-business African American therapist.

To tell the truth, all I had going for me during those first few sessions with Pete was my ethical obligation to "do no harm" and my practical commitment to keep my job. Underneath those intentions, I was aware of my feelings of disdain as I watched Pete's blustering demeanor with other patients on the unit. At first, it took every ounce of professionalism I could muster to sit, listen, and engage with him—sometimes through silent expressiveness, and other times through genuine questions. I did not have to like him; I did have to let him know that I would not intentionally humiliate him.

As we sat through those sessions together, something else started to emerge in our relationship. I became curious about Pete. What made him who he was? The more curious I became, the safer he felt. I too became safer in the relationship, less determined to protect my story, less needful of the emotional armor I used to defend my racial dignity and professional boundaries. The safer he felt, the more easily I could see the sad young man who was struggling to reclaim his playfulness, as well as his sincere desire to matter in the world. I witnessed the same process of respect toward Pete unfolding in the patient group, a racially diverse group of women and men all struggling with drugs, all helping each other uncover bits of humanity long buried under the detritus of their addictions. Over time, the experience of respect allowed Pete to show up, without his metaphorical robes, and engage the journey toward recovery. Prior to getting to know Pete, my story of who I was as a Black woman did not include coming to care about someone who donned sheets and hoods to terrorize Black people.

Respect starts with listening in order to let go of dualistic perceptions. We all carry stories in our heads and hearts about who we think we are. What is interesting about those stories is that they include both a *Model Me* narrative—how we want to be seen in the world—and a *Not Me* narrative.

My *Model Me* on that hospital unit with Pete needed to be in complete control: intellectually superior and emotionally invincible, especially when dealing with the "Petes" of the world. My Not Me was an easily duped or overwhelmed neophyte. I could not be vulnerable, and neither could I be goaded into acting unprofessionally by a stronger-willed Klansman. In other words, I started with no higher hope than to win in my interactions with Pete, not to heal or to grow. I had trapped myself and Pete in what the author Chimamanda Ngozi Adichie (2009) calls "the danger of a single story." Respect meant acknowledging that there are always multiple and sometimes contradictory stories behind the emotion-grabbing headlines.

Five Questions to Foster Respect. One way to fortify the disposition of respect is to ask ourselves these critical questions.

1. What is the goal of the encounter: to silence the other or to prove ourselves right?
2. Do I want to "win" by converting the other person to my point of view? (*The desire to win may be rooted in benign intent, such as pushing someone to accept your analysis of a problem and recommendation of solution.*)
3. What is happening that is triggering intense feelings in me?
4. Am I personally under attack? (*By personal, I don't mean just "individual." Personal includes loyalty to another person or group.*)
5. Am I processing feelings around non-negotiable values? Am I experiencing moral outrage? (*You know you are experiencing moral outrage when you have a "how could you!" moment. Notice that moral outrage is a condemnation, not a request for information.*)

The responses that emerge will clue you in to your "Model Me" or preferred identity narrative: how you want to be seen in the world. They will also provide insight into your Not Me narrative.

Chances are your Not Me narrative is implicated in how you see the other person, especially when you view that person as Utterly Other. These identity narratives can erode the foundation of respect necessary for empathic engagement. Meeting Pete and getting to know him beyond the single voice narrative that showed up on television was an important passage in my personal and professional growth. We were both, and I like to think other participant-patients as well, presented with an opportunity to expand our constricted narratives of Self and take steps, however tentative, to move toward a larger vision of human possibility.

The Third Pillar in the ARC of Empathy: Compassion

There is a quote often attributed to Buddhist monk Thich Nhat Hanh (2014): "Our great task in life is to awaken from the illusion of separation." Our indivisibility is now an established scientific fact. Physiological events and psychological processes we once considered to be strictly private have been shown to be "contagious": Our mirror neurons enable us to read each other's intentions. Our interactions momentarily alter the structure and function of each other's brains. In short, our interdependence is hardwired.

Compassion, intentional acknowledgment of that shared humanity, is a choice. To paraphrase a consistent theme in the work of psychotherapist Sheldon Kopp, we choose compassion when we engage another person, knowing that for all apparent differences we are interconnected, a part of the same human fabric. While this definition may sound ethereal, it is hard, hands-on work, not the least of which is letting go of the dualisms at the core of our stories—our feeling-thoughts about who we think we are.

We reinforce the illusion of separateness with story lines we tell ourselves to develop a Model Me and a Not Me. Similarly, the illusion of separateness is sustained with dualistic story lines about others, often culminating with relegating some person or group of people to Utterly Other, the very antithesis of who we think we are. To be truthful, almost all of us this very second can think of some person or maybe a group whom we experience as Utterly Other. Once formed, the category of Utterly Other provides tangible justification that humanity can be divided into people who are deserving and people who are not. It is this question that drives the policies and practices that determine access to goods and resources, both material and relational. Who deserves safe drinking water? Who deserves access to an environment free of toxic pollutants? Who deserves medicine to sustain health and life? Another chance? A kind smile? This kind of dualism bolsters the ideologies that have undergirded racial stratification from the inception of this country. To choose compassion is to counteract these dualistic impulses. The work is straightforward and simple, but not at all easy.

The Best of Enemies. I can think of a no more beautiful example of the work of compassion than that illustrated by the lives and love of Ann Atwater, a Black public housing activist, and C. P. Ellis, a former Exalted Cyclops of the Ku Klux Klan. As their story is told in the bestselling book by Osha Gray Davidson (*The Best of Enemies*, 1996), Atwater and Ellis both grew up in Durham, NC, a culture where deeply entrenched racial segregation was the way of life, defining the narratives of identity and possibility: this is who you are and this is all you can become.

C. P. Ellis grew up as a poor White boy, who regularly witnessed his father's humiliation when he had to step off the sidewalk so that the "big White men"—men with money—could pass. He grew up hiding under stairwells, so that his schoolmates wouldn't see that all he had to eat for lunch was a lard sandwich. But he became a "somebody." He, like his father before him, was eventually inducted into the Ku Klux Klan, and he rose to leadership as the Exalted Cyclops. Ann Atwater grew up poor and Black and female in this same culture. She was deeply intimate with the indignities of being poor and Black and female—all of which according to the cultural narrative would relegate her to a status of nobody-ness. But she too became "somebody." She became one of Durham's most audacious and outspoken advocates for civil rights; she was a single mother and housing activist who could not be silenced.

In Ellis's words, this is how they encountered each other:

> Here we are, two people from the far end of the fence, having identical problems, except her being black and me being white . . . The amazing thing about it, her and I, up to that point, [had] cussed each other, bawled each other, we hated each other. Up to that point, we didn't know each other. We didn't know we had things in common. (Korstad & Leloudis, 2010, p. 317)

Over the course of years and with the help of an orchestrated process known as a charrette, Atwater and Ellis learned to listen to the multiple and sometimes conflicting truths that each had lived and needed to tell. Through that listening, they found themselves in each other. When Atwater delivered a eulogy at Ellis's funeral in 2005, she took her rightful place alongside his family, saying "I have lost a brother" (Brown, 2019).

Aside from the heart-touching story of their shared journey (Ellis eventually shredded his KKK membership card), we can derive three lessons from the lives of Atwater and Ellis. First, compassion does not require sameness or attraction. It is not compassion that requires another person to live by our terms; that is ego-augmentation. Compassion does not require us to agree with, condone, or find another person's (or our own) behavior the least bit acceptable. We can stand firmly in our own shoes, uphold our values and convictions, and still find that liminal space—a gentle, open space that makes room for another person's becoming.

Five Questions to Choose Compassion. To choose compassion is to foster relational courage. These five questions can help.

1. How did this person come to be where she is right now in this relationship?
2. What aspects of humanity is this encounter revealing?
3. What feeling-thoughts are emerging as I witness this humanity?
4. What turn of events in in my life might have led me to believe, speak, or behave similarly?
5. Under what conditions do I believe, speak, and behave similarly?

Therapist and author Sheldon Kopp (1972) once wrote that he makes it his practice to look for himself inside his clients. The younger me found this practice incredible—perhaps even foolhardy. Now I understand his comment as an affirmation of our shared humanity. I also take it to mean that compassion is the antidote to contempt. Disruptive empathy is never an assurance of comfort, nor should it be. By definition, it is an unsettling process, but one that guarantees safety from contempt and condemned isolation.

A STORY I WOULD RATHER NOT TELL

And now for a story I would rather not tell, but I must. When I moved to the Boston area in the early 1990s, it took a while for me to adapt to the vicissitudes of New England winters. One January night, I found myself on a train heading to a commitment in the city, thinking at the same time that most sane people were home sheltered against the blowing ice and snow. Only a few of us hardy or foolhardy souls were on the train; the conductor and I were the only Black women on the train. Somewhere along the route she and I fell into the kind of friendly chatter that instantiates superficial bonding. In other words, we probably talked about nothing more meaningful than the blowing snow. Yet I was warmed and grateful for our brief interaction. As we drew near the Boston downtown area, she pulled to a stop where a Chinese woman stepped onto the train. The would-be passenger's spoken English was halting at best, and she didn't have the correct change. In a very harsh tone, the conductor informed her that she couldn't board the train, all of the while glancing at me.

I was aware that the conductor was demonstrating her absolute power and was looking to me for affirmation. That's when I wimped out. I was afraid to look at the conductor, nor was I able to look at the poor woman she was mistreating. I eventually summoned the courage to take the exact change from my purse to hand to the woman. But I was too late. Before I could reach her, she exited the train back into the ice and blowing snow. For the rest of the trip, I could feel the conductor looking at me, but this time it was a steely glare. As feeble and ineffectual as my action had been, I had betrayed the conductor and our presumed racialized bond.

Within a span of about 15 minutes, I succumbed to the major cultural force that deconstructs our hardwired capacity for empathy: tribal loyalty. Based only on an ephemeral and superficial bond with a woman I would likely never see again, I failed to help another woman when I clearly could have. What went unspoken between the conductor and me was the mutual understanding that, as Black women, we were much maligned in the dominant culture. Here was our chance to exact revenge (by proxy) for our subjugation, to assert our dominance over a third woman, who was likely an immigrant who was not fluent in English. On the face of things, the train conductor was upholding a facially neutral policy. However, the intent behind her scrupulous compliance was racially malevolent, and for far too long I sat in a state of moral paralysis, unable to do what I knew needed to be done.

The effects of race on helping behavior has been widely documented; much to my ongoing dismay, I enacted findings published by researchers such as Gaertner, Dovidio, and Johnson (1982), who have been publishing for the past 3 decades. Specifically, we succumb to conformity pressures and fail to help a different-race bystander in the presence of passive witnesses. Gaertner, Dovidio, and Johnson's initial study questioned a hypothesis about cross-racial helping behaviors when the victim was Black. Using biotelemetry, they found that the inhibition effect was due to normative pressures not to intervene.

In my case, I risked nothing more than the fleeting disapproval of a Black woman whom I did not know. However, risk of extrusion from whatever transitory tribe I might belong to was enough to temporarily disengage my moral compass. To be sure, we encounter other barriers to empathy along the way, but I would be remiss not to name this one as a toxic dynamic that has the potential to disrupt every social interaction, from the most mundane to the most consequential.

Disruptive empathy is not mushy stuff. Neither is it for the faint of heart. As Jordan has argued over the years, and most recently in her republished *Relational-Cultural Therapy* (2017), empathy requires tremendous ego strength. However, ego strength must not be interpreted as ego for the sake of preserving or augmenting ego. It is not cultivated by constricted relational images that impose limits and limitations on who we can become and how we choose to be in this world. Our neural hardwiring supports the cultivation of empathy, and it is a capacity that must be practiced, particularly when there are cultural forces (e.g., racialized hierarchies) that actively undermine the practice of empathy.

REFLECTIONS

Draw a picture or write a character sketch of your "Model Me" (a racialized angel). How would it look? What qualities are you proud of—qualities that you are proud to say: "This is the kind of person I am"?

When is your "Model Me" likely to show up? What happens next?

How about your "Not Me" (a racialized demon)? What are the qualities that you never want others to see in you—qualities that you never like to see in yourself? When is your "Not Me" likely to show up? What happens next?

CHAPTER 7

Mindful Authenticity

Tell all the truth, but tell it slant—

. . .

The truth must dazzle gradually
Or every man be blind.

—Emily Dickinson

Few of us want to be intentionally *dis*honest about race. However, given the nature of our racialized histories and lifestyles, the thought of having an honest conversation about race is likely to trigger a range of stress responses—from attack and defend to avoid and dissemble. As much as we profess to value honesty, we all know that much harm can be done when honesty is a camouflage for verbal brutishness. And in an era that places high value on "keeping it real," we are often suspicious not only of the measured speech that prosody demands, but of the indirection that telling it slant implies and the slow accumulation of truth that dazzles gradually.

Instead, we become adept at using code-speak to talk about race, not only to mask discrimination, as discussed in Chapter 5, but to tamp down anxiety. Sometimes code-speak can take the form of sanitized, but ultimately nonsensical euphemisms, for example, terms such as "urban" or "inner city" signal race, not geography. At other times, code-speak (e.g., political dog whistles) have a more nefarious function. As Republican political consultant Lee Atwater notoriously advised his clients in 1981, saying "nigger" is likely to backfire against public opinion, so using phrases such as "states' rights" and "forced busing" would have to suffice to promote a racist agenda (Perlstein, 2012). In these instances, code-speak provides cover by making otherwise unacceptable language acceptable.

In other words, race and racism are shame-ridden topics, and it's no wonder that we worry about "saying the wrong thing." We want to avoid the discomfort (or danger) of offending someone, as well as the discomfort of being offended. In an effort to stave off uneasiness or embarrassment we resort to code-speak, language that is vague enough to be generally palatable, even if non-illuminating. In these instances, words like "diversity" and "minority" function as catch-all phrases to signal "not White" without ever saying brown or black or any other physical marker of race. It is as if there is a tacit pact of nondisclosure that enables us to survive, rather than grow and thrive in relationship. Unfortunately, neither the dog whistles nor the euphemisms move us closer to the truths of our humanity: who we think we are or who we believe we can become. Nor do they help us connect more authentically with each other.

MINDFUL AUTHENTICITY

There is another way: a relational anchoring practice that I call mindful authenticity. Before I go into a more detailed description of how this practice works (and—just as important—how it doesn't work), let's review a basic definition derived from RCT. In her 2010 volume on Relational-Cultural Therapy, Jordan defines authenticity as the capacity to bring one's real experience, feelings, and thoughts into relationship with sensitivity and awareness of the possible impact of one's actions or expressions on others (p. 101).

In other words, "keeping it real" might best be reframed as staying present and aware of multiple realities as they emerge in relationship. It is in fact the antithesis of self-absorbed reactivity. Mindful authenticity requires cultivating the capacity for truth telling without losing sight of the other person's humanity.

THE THREE C MINDSET

Underlying the practice of mindful authenticity is what I call the Three C Mindset: complexity, courage, and consideration. Singly, each takes time and thoughtfulness to master; together, they offer us a way to talk honestly and openly about race. The scenarios presented in the next part of this chapter will more fully illustrate these perspectives.

Complexity

The complexity mindset starts with acknowledgment that we all live multistoried lives. There is more to each of us than the "face," the story that is most readily seen by others, or the face we most readily present to others. Some of these are stories primarily of our own making, our preferred narratives. It typically doesn't take much prompting for any of us to launch into one-line descriptions of ourselves.

"I am a liberal Democrat."
"I am a proud African American."
"I am not racist."

"I speak truth to power."
"I believe in pro-life values."

You get the broad-brush picture. The issue is not whether these statements are true, it's that they represent a thinly drawn depiction of how we want to be seen in the world.

Toward the end of my doctoral studies, I sat with one of my academic supervisors. As we reviewed one of my final comprehensive papers (a 2-day test that involved sitting in a windowless room writing in ink—no erasures allowed), I was mortified to find glaring grammatical errors. "That's not me!" I indignantly exclaimed. I preferred to see myself as a highly educated African American woman who would not countenance disagreement between subjects and verbs!

To which he replied: "Of course it is. It's you under stress."

With that quiet response, my supervisor prompted me not only to contextualize my self-image, but to notice my emotional investment in that image. Now you might say it's only grammar, and you would be partly right. The rest of the story would be that in my early childhood, I had been tutored by my mother and affirmed by elementary school teachers for speaking proper grammar. It was not just a matter of education; it was a matter of racial dignity. It was both my filial and tribal obligation to defy any racial stereotype that threatened to confirm our "less than" educational status in the world. Imagine my chagrin then at being exposed to my White supervisor as someone who didn't always write grammatically perfect prose.

A complexity mindset prompts us to loosen our grip on the images we bring into relationship, both within and across racialized descriptions. As you might imagine, it is our emotional and political attachment to these images that can lead to toxic conflict. It's not that we should refrain from these "one-liners." But we should always have the courage to ask ourselves: Under what circumstances is this true? When is it not true? What else is true about me?

Courage

There is a type of "what if" question that can infuse any relationship with fear, and makes it that much harder to talk about race.

What if I am wrong?
What if someone disrespects me?
What if I am misunderstood?
What if I make her angry?

Without a mindset grounded in courage, these questions can have a deadening effect on any relationship. Sometimes we feel as if our brains have just shut down. We freeze or deflect. At other times, we may just try to power through, or use our words to overpower. In those cases, we may end up saying things that we later regret.

Courage is not fearlessness; it is openness to uncertainty. Put another way, it is the capacity to act meaningfully and with integrity in the face of acknowledged vulnerability (Jordan, 1990). I like to think of courage as the willingness to be imperfect and vulnerable. That means we won't always have the right words.

There will be times, when confronted with racialized conflicts, that our thoughts will be as muddled as our histories. Moreover, one consequence of living in a culture given to stratifying people into winners and losers is that our interactions too are measured and ranked. While we may not approach an encounter with the conscious goal of "winning" the conversation, we almost reflexively protect ourselves from feeling like a loser. In other words, we use our relational images—our "stories" as protective armor in relationships. The experience of uncertainty—being at a loss for words—may then feel like a gaping hole in that armor that we must defend at any cost.

Contrary to conventional notions, the capacity to tolerate uncertainty is the essence of authenticity. The English poet John Keats dubbed this quality as negative capability: the willingness to embrace uncertainty, live with mystery, and make peace with ambiguity without irritable grasping after fact and reason (Popova, n.d.).

Translating this notion into clinical practice, RCT scholar and practitioner Roseann Adams described negative capability as willingness to enter into MUD with each other: mystery, uncertainty, and doubt (unpublished transcript, Jean Baker Miller Training Institute, Spring 2010). Similarly, as RCT scholars Miller and Stiver (1995) insisted, authenticity requires movement toward real relationship, not fearful clinging to image. It follows that negative capability is what 21st-century philosophers and practitioners of healing therapies call "presence." From this perspective, authenticity is more about being in the present than "keeping it real." To be present to emerging realities in the context of "what is" is to be at once thoughtful and vulnerable—a daunting practice that is nearly impossible without a mindset of courage.

Consideration

The third aspect of the Three C Mindset is consideration. Consideration might be best described as intentionality about the purpose, context, and timing of an interaction. We never know when someone might make a comment that offends our sensibilities or behave in a way that violates our sense of right and wrong. For example, we could be sitting around a holiday dinner table when Uncle Gene makes a racist comment about slavery, or Aunt Millie opines that good, hard-working White people shouldn't have to pay high health-care costs for ghetto teenagers who can't stop having babies. Such comments might set off a heavy pounding in your heart and head, and you might feel the need to deliver a sharp retort. After all, Uncle Gene and Aunt Millie can't be allowed to serve up their toxic beliefs at the dinner table. If you can't "do nothing," what can you do? How? When? And for what purpose?

Chances are, their racist comments notwithstanding, Uncle Gene and Aunt Millie are decent human beings. Uncle Gene might be a volunteer for ASPCA, while Aunt Millie regularly visits sick and shut-in members of her church community. Like the rest of us, their comments and viewpoints about racialized politics are forged in the crucible of their own identity narratives. As such, they are likely not amenable to change through precise logic or emotion-driven censure. In fact, we now know that addressing emotionally charged arguments with "pure logic" is like adding fuel to fire. The response to such logic is likely to be ever-deepening entrenchment. Similarly, responding with a scathing retort—or fighting fire with fire—will result only in heat and escalating toxicity.

Consideration, in this case, might be called anticipatory empathy: pausing to consider how a comment will land or what kind of emotional reaction a comment might trigger (Jordan, 2010). If the answer to that question is "I don't care," you have a clue to your purpose. You may simply want to shut them down or vent off steam. If, on the other hand, your purpose is to open a possibility for more thoughtful and clarifying interactions, and/or you have a genuine relationship with Aunt Millie and Uncle Gene, anticipatory empathy is a must. It facilitates what is known in RCT literature as a growth-fostering relationship: one in which all participants have an opportunity to grow.

Consideration means asking yourself questions. Is now the time and place? What kinds of conversations are possible while passing mashed potatoes and cranberry sauce? Clearly, consideration of purpose, time, and context obviates any impulse toward a quick fix. It requires presence of mind and a commitment to courage. Fortunately, having a large mammalian brain means that we are not captive to every fleeting impulse, no matter how adept Uncle Gene and Aunt Millie may be in triggering amygdala reactivity. Mindful authenticity is a skill that we can cultivate and a choice we can make even in the most challenging of circumstances.

Let's recap. Mindful authenticity is an anchoring relational practice because it promotes awareness of complexity, intention, and timeliness. It cultivates thoughtfulness and normalizes vulnerability, thus loosening our attachment to image and our fearful allegiance to identity narratives. Anchored by this practice, we are more able to show up in the relationship that is in front of us.

MINDFUL AUTHENTICITY AND SELF-DISCLOSURE

To illustrate more deeply how mindful authenticity can work, let's look at an example from my clinical practice. During the first year, I had a client whom I sometimes refer to as Brad. An African American graduate student, Brad often made brutally disparaging comments about his academic advisor, also an African American male. When I questioned Brad about his relationship with this man, he explained that he didn't so much dislike him as mistrust him. His advisor, he explained, was married to a White woman, and he could never trust a Black man who had a White wife. Brad claimed that he had never found a White woman attractive, with the possible exception of the movie star Julia Roberts.

I thought to myself, indeed this gentleman doth protest too much. However, with this explanation, Brad ushered us into a critical juncture in our new relationship; my job was to decide how to be present in it. I considered a couple of scenarios: one, that Brad already knew that I was in a mixed-race marriage and was "poking" for a reaction; or two, that he didn't know but was testing my racial-political sensibilities.

Mindful authenticity is about making choices—knowing that there is more than one right way to do the right thing. It also means that doing the right thing can be done in a way that is less than helpful to the relationship. One choice—what some might deem the right thing from a strictly therapeutic stance—would have been to disclose my personal information right away. The rationale underlying this choice was that nondisclosure might be experienced as "therapist neutrality," a nonresponsive posture that is often an impediment to healing (Jordan, 2004).

However, I also needed to consider how Brad would experience such a revelation in this new relationship at that precise moment. My primary concern was that Brad might experience my disclosure as shaming and unduly confrontational. Given the power differential in our relationship, it was not unthinkable that Brad would feel as if I was "putting him in his place" had I interjected. (*Who likes to be caught with his foot jammed into his mouth? Imagine how it feels when the only options are to backtrack, to apologize, or to defend?*) For the time being, I decided to say nothing to Brad about my marriage to a White man.

In this scenario, whether or not I would disclose was not so much the issue as when and how I would do so. Because I decided to postpone disclosure, our relationship led to thoughtful conversations about the personal and political challenges of cross-racial intimacy. My eventual and later disclosure was made in the context of a relationship between two people who were becoming more fully known to each other. This process enabled Brad to freely explore his ambivalence about his racial identity, as well as his conflictual experiences as a bisexual male in a heteronormative society.

When we talked later about his experience of our process, Brad said that he appreciated the fact that I didn't "call him out" for what could have been an offensive remark. He went on to say that the more our relationship developed over a 3-week period the less relevant the specific content seemed. Then he laughed and said he "suspected" I was in a mixed relationship because I once mentioned eating lobster in Maine. "Lobster and Maine," he said, "usually involves White folks."

MINDFUL AUTHENTICITY AND PRODUCTIVE CONFLICT

Mindful authenticity can be a welcoming portal into productive conflict. Though often associated with the problematic aspects of relationship, conflict without power-over maneuvering is an essential source of growth. When cast in terms of winning and losing as in a zero-sum game, conflict quite readily devolves into combat. Here's what I mean. In a power-over relationship, participants are cast into presumably permanent roles of domination and subordination. Inasmuch as productive conflict entails clear and courageous expression of needs, persons in the dominant group may work to suppress such expression. Some of the silencing tactics (which will be discussed in more detail in later chapters) are minimization, denigration, deflection, and threat. In other words, false harmony serves the interest of the dominant group.

Productive conflict, on the other hand, invites different-ness into the relationship as an opportunity for expansion and clarification. Mary Parker Follett (1951) described this process as "creating relationship" (p. 128). In her seminal work *Toward a New Psychology of Women*, Miller (1976) described the process as "waging good conflict." To be able to move into good conflict entails a well-differentiated sense of one's reality and the willingness to represent one's needs and concerns within relationship (Jordan, 1990). Further, the intention to wage good conflict enables participants to "center" the relationship—that is, to transcend any impulse to "have one's own way" by silencing or otherwise vanquishing the other. The long-term health of the relationship becomes a priority.

ONE TRUE THING

Jean Baker Miller emphasized the necessity of good conflict to spur growth. However, as a 1st-year practicing psychologist and the first African American clinician in Harvard Business School's counseling service, I was not looking for opportunities to "wage good conflict" with anyone. Of course, growth opportunities happen whether we want them or not. As you may recall from Chapter 4, Ken, "The Boss," presented me with one such opportunity. When

Ken strode into my office, a tall, well-muscled, 20-something White male, I was immediately struck by his attire: a starched white shirt, neatly pressed khakis, and expertly buffed leather shoes. When he took a seat, crossed his legs, and folded his arms across his chest, I knew that if pictures speak a thousand words, his body language spoke volumes more. He dispelled any doubt when he looked at me sternly and said, "Well, what can I do for you?" Who knows—he might have meant to ask: "How should I start?" or "What do I need to tell you?" However, he began by attempting to reverse roles, effectively suppressing any sense of his own vulnerability. That made complete sense to me. I could identify with the trepidation of walking into a counselor's office for the first time. Although I was a bit shaken by his blatant attempt to be in "control," I put on my game face (a reassuring smile) and tried a rather generic—and I thought, nonthreatening—opening. It went something like: "Why don't we start by talking a bit about your decision to make the appointment." Because I already had a sense of unease with this young man, I silently congratulated myself on my apparent smoothness.

Ken quickly popped that self-satisfied bubble. He leaned forward, looked me in the eye and said: "Let's get one thing clear. I am a White, male, conservative Republican. I'm not one of you people who believe other people should solve your problems."

Let me describe just a few of the thoughts that surfaced through the momentary cognitive fog I slipped into upon hearing those words. First, the sensation: Heat began rising through my body. Then the impulse: I wanted to smack him down, if not physically, certainly verbally. Next came the escape route: Perhaps I could slough him off to someone else in the office—a White male colleague—since Ken and I were obviously not a good fit. Then the diminution and self-doubt: "Am I not good enough to be here," followed by indignation: "*Who does he think he is!?*"

Fortunately, in those 20 seconds of silence, two other thoughts surfaced. One was my ethical obligation to "do no harm." That obligation eliminated the "smack down" option. The second was advice gleaned from psychologist and mentor Irene Stiver (1990): In the face of a potential impasse, say one true thing. With as much respect as I could muster in the moment, I remembered to say one true thing: "It must have taken a great deal of courage for you to come to talk to me today."

Within seconds, Ken began to weep as he shared the painful dilemma that led him to seek help. As you can see, "one true thing" is not a perfect utterance. It is also not the only true thing that might be spoken. It is, in effect, a statement of acknowledgment and respect: a truth that allows fuller truths to emerge in relationship.

The practice of authenticity reminds me of a quote attributed to Sufi poet Rumi: "In between notions of right doing and wrong-doing, there is a field. I will meet you there" (Rumi, 2004). Saying one true thing places us in the middle of that field, and three things happen there. First, the speaker is able to preserve her or his own integrity. There is no false humility or self-abnegation. Second, the speaker acknowledges the reality of the other person. There is no attempt to deny, change, minimize, or otherwise suppress the other's perspective. Third, the speaker conveys confidence in the relationship as a space that can hold conflict: a space where people can explore their narratives of difference, identity, and possibility.

SHOWING UP FOR YOUR OWN TRUTH

In addition to saying one true thing, there are other anchoring practices that facilitate clarity and movement toward new possibilities in relationship. However, before delineating these practices, let me share one final illustrative scenario. My perennial mentor, "David," and his wife gave a small dinner party for a group of friends, all of whom had retired from very successful careers. All of the people gathered around the table were White. As the conversation turned more political over the course of the evening, one guest opined that the Black boys in their saggy britches hanging out in the street were going nowhere fast. He went on: "They would be better off as slaves."

This story was related to me by David's wife, who said that David remained silent, choosing not to respond directly to the comment. The evening ended, the guests went home, the hosts debriefed the evening—including their disbelief at the vehemence of their colleague's racial bigotry. I suspect, though I was not told, that they might have wondered why their guest chose to vent that particular viewpoint in their home. David was well known throughout the area as a racial justice activist: In the 1960s he participated in civil rights marches and provided sanctuary for leaders such as Dr. Martin Luther King, Jr. In addition to his work as a wealth manager in the 1980s, he funded and established a museum to preserve, promote, and celebrate African American history and culture. Could it be that the guest was baiting him? (A glass of wine or two might induce that kind of disinhibited behavior.)

David opted for consideration. He waited, allowed himself time to sort through his reactions of hurt and anger, and then telephoned his colleague a day or two after the dinner party. Perhaps he acknowledged what we call "gray areas"—places that are part of an individual's certainties, thereby opening an attitudinal space for new information and awareness and for widening the perspectival lens. David may have located parts of himself that were not in *agreement* with his colleague's conclusions, but helped him to understand his motivations. He might have recalled times or circumstances when the young men in their droopy pants triggered similar feelings of fear and disdain.

When David finally made the call to his colleague, he expressed not only his disagreement, but also his disappointment and worry about the impact of such bigotry in the world. Importantly, the purpose of David's call was *not* to convince the other person of his wrong-headedness or demand that he change. Nor was David motivated to proclaim his superior virtue or overwhelm with his hard-won wisdom. Instead, the purpose of his call was to stand up for his own clear-headed, whole-hearted truths without violating the dignity of another human being.

That's when something very interesting happened: His colleague apologized and thanked him. He went on to say that he appreciated the fact that David confronted him directly. He felt moved by the fact that David had not chosen to excoriate him to other people or attempt to banish him from their circle of colleagues. David's discussion about race had managed to keep it real without becoming verbally brutal. He had allowed the truth to gradually emerge.

DOING AUTHENTICITY: FOUR SIMPLE PRACTICES

In addition to consideration, showing up and representing his truths, David modeled four other practices that are integral to mindful authenticity. Below are four anchoring practices that facilitate clarity and movement toward new possibilities in relationship.

1. First, pause; take a breath or several breaths. Allow sufficient time to respond while in a relaxed body state. It is nearly impossible to be reactive when we are relaxed, and the opposite is also true. It is nearly impossible to be responsive when we are tense and "braced" for conflict. While it sounds counterintuitive and is definitely countercultural, mindful authenticity requires that we soften—allow our muscles to relax for conflict.

2. *Notice your feeling-thoughts—all of them.* Listen to the voices in your head and the beating of your heart. Presence in relationship is a full-bodied, whole-brain experience. Being clearheaded, or thinking straight, includes awareness and respect for your emotions. Listening to all of the voices does not mean speaking them out loud. It is instead a level of relational discernment: representation in relationship that is at once choiceful and truthful.

3. *Let go of any need to win.* Usually in conversations about race, each party wants to either convert or silence the other—sometimes using lessons from history, statistical data, personal experience, logic, moral precepts, or some combination of all these.

4. *Let go of any notion of a "perfect finish."* Conversations about race are rarely "one and done." In other words, do not expect these large, emotionally fraught issues to be resolved once and for all.

HOLDING CONTRADICTORY TRUTHS

Truth is rarely static, and it can be most untidy. Truth needs breathing room. In his book *Letting Stories Breathe*, Frank (2010) emphasizes the need to respect the multiple subjectivities embedded in each voice. When we allow our narratives about self and other to breathe, we come to see that our stories are intertextual.

I was standing by my mother's graveside when a weeping, 60-something-year-old White man whom I had never met told me that he kept a picture of himself standing between my mother and his mother. The caption read "My Two Mamas." He knew my mother as Mary; I knew her as Mom. She had worked as a domestic in his home for over 50 years.

Two truths emerged. We had both grown up coming to know ourselves through our relationship with this woman, *and* we did not know the same woman. That said, I cannot use my story to impugn the integrity of his story. What's more, his story of becoming deeply intersected with my own. The Mary who cooked his holiday dinners was the Mom who was missing from my table at home. Upon meeting him, my grief had to expand to include his as well.

We come to realize that our lives are always in process—acts of cocreation that are too complex to fit within the confines of any one small story. Further, there is no such thing as "the truth, the whole truth, and nothing but the truth" except on 1960s television shows. Remember Banaji's "mind bugs"? We don't always know what we don't know. Neither do we know all of the externalities that shape our story of who we are in the world. However, one outcome of mindful authenticity is that sometimes contradictory truths emerge in relationship. In relationship our stories help us to become more fully aware of who we are and what choices we have about who we are becoming.

REFLECTIONS

What, for you, is the most challenging aspect of mindful authenticity? During instances of racialized conflict, which parts of your experience might you withhold or under-express? Which might you over-express? Which of the practices mentioned in this chapter might help you develop the Three C Mindset?

Recall a time when someone made a racially offensive comment that left you at a loss for words. If you were to revisit that situation (or if a similar situation occurs in the future), what is one true thing you might say to stay present in the situation?

CHAPTER 8

Dynamic Mutuality

Empowering Action in Relationship

> . . . all the powers
> and principalities of alienation
> collapse   and crumble
> just because we dare to
> see
> each other
> eyes to eyes.

> —William D. Larkin III

For decades I was convinced that I along with everyone else had a True Self. To Western ears, the notion of a True Self really isn't all that strange until we begin to articulate it. It goes something like this. True Self is a pristine, immutable, and encapsulated quality. Although we may not think of True Self as having material form, we do imagine True Self as having a location somewhere deep inside, waiting—first to be discovered, then courageously enacted, and finally protected. It is as if we believe that True Self is a "Real Thing."

With its emphasis on the Separate Self, True Self took shape in my imagination as an accretion of images that were disconnected, or at the very least, extrapolated from relationship. Interestingly, this accretion of images (aka True Self) tends to consist of highly favorable self-descriptions. In other words, we like to think of True Self as pure—untainted by historical, socio-economic, ethnic, or racial realities.

ACTION IN RELATIONSHIP

In contrast, Jean Baker Miller (1976) theorized that we come to know who we are through action in relationship, through encounters with embodied difference. When I first read Miller's "action in relationship" thesis, it resonated deeply on both a poetic and intellectual level.

However, personal resonance is a somewhat more fraught experience. Once formed, favorable self-narratives can be resistant to change. Let me explain what I mean by relating a series of encounters with an African American gentleman, a "friend" I will call Edwin.

I say "friend" in quotes and can call him Edwin because I never asked his name, nor did I offer to tell him mine. My relationship with Edwin can only be described as paradoxical: He occupied a place of significance and marginality in my life.

Every morning, rain or shine, cold or hot, Edwin stood in the middle of a snarly intersection acting as an unofficial traffic director while collecting money from commuters (presumably making their way to their city offices). He was gray-bearded, walked with a limp, and his open smile revealed several missing teeth. He wore a laminated sign around his neck that read: *Help the Homeless Mission*. I didn't know if he was homeless, or if any such mission actually existed. I just knew I liked him and felt very proud of myself every time I deposited a dollar or two in his collection can.

Of course, I also noticed that other people passed by without giving a donation, and still others seemed irritated by Edwin's presence. They were my "Not Me" people—usually White, stern-faced males, who were presumably off to do some non–socially conscious work. Just as I had constructed a narrative about myself, I had constructed a counter-narrative about them as well. The "I" of my True Self was a socially conscious, sympathetic-to-homeless-people, kind-hearted African American woman. They were politically conservative, class-privileged, probably racially intolerant White men.

For 6 or 7 years, I would encounter Edwin in the traffic circle. He would greet me with an enthusiastic "Hey Darling!" or "How's it going, Baby Girl?" I would respond with chitchat about weather or some inane topic while we waited for the lights to change or for the traffic to unsnarl in some other mysterious way. One day, as I approached the intersection I noticed that I didn't have my dollars handy, and worse, my purse was in the back seat. First, I hoped I could slide through the intersection without being seen, since he was behind me engaging with other commuters. As I scrambled desperately, hoping to find an errant dollar or at least change on the floor or in the seat crevices, I noticed him limping toward my car. I was caught without money. Worse, Edwin saw me looking for money. He said: "Hey, Baby Girl. I just want to holler at you and say good morning. You don't owe me nothing." He asserted himself as a human being who was greeting me, just another human being. In that moment I became aware that I had constructed an entirely transactional exchange, one that bolstered my self-image. Mercifully, the light changed, and I managed a wan smile and greeting before escaping through the intersection and into the city. Edwin had invaded my comfort zone and upended my self-righteous Model Me narrative. I now had to amend my story of myself, of Edwin, and of the people around us.

What did I learn? For starters, I would say that I learned about the importance of shared power in respectful relationships with other people. For many years, I had positioned Edwin in my story as a necessary prop; his only role was to help me maintain my favorable image of myself. As Wexler (2006) suggested in *Brain and Culture*, forcing another person to exist inside a narrative not of their own making is an enactment of power-over.

In contrast, dynamic mutuality admits the possibility of being transformed by someone who may exist in our imaginations as "Not Me" or "Utterly Other." In her writings on mutuality, Jordan (2002, 2010) delineates these aspects of the dynamic mutuality experience: interest in the other person as a whole person; emotional accessibility; receptivity; and active initiative. This definition is interactional, emphasizing the power of all persons to be present and active in the relationship flow. Dynamic mutuality consists of willingness to influence and to be influenced by the other participants in relationship.

Interestingly, this definition is aligned with Miller's concept of power as a relational energy that induces responsiveness: the capacity to move and be moved by another. When we are willing to be influenced by another, including or especially those persons we deem to be unlike ourselves, hard-line boundaries soften and become more permeable. Furthermore, we are able to assess our own experience with more clarity.

As I left the intersection that morning, my encounter with Edwin surfaced questions and previously ignored realities. One was that Edwin was not the only "homeless" person in that intersection. Other women and men of various ethnicities were standing in the traffic with similarly vague signage. The difference was simple: Edwin was the one I liked. Until he showed up and asserted himself as a real person, he was little more than a "nice old Black man" image. I could fit him into my story of how Model Me interacts with "People Like Him."

This recognition led to other questions. Why did I not object to his easy familiarity? I not only tolerated, I actually enjoyed his "nicknames" for me: Baby Doll, Sugar, Baby Girl, and Sunshine. Had he not been Black, presumably poor, and possibly older than I, would I have indulged what I typically define as sexist language? Or was it simply that the accretion of "Not Me" images meant that he did not matter, that I did not respect him as enough of a whole person to be indignant?

UNDERSTANDING AND MISUNDERSTANDING DYNAMIC MUTUALITY

Mutuality is a core principle of Relational-Cultural practice. It is also a word that lands softly on the ear, perhaps because it sounds like a term that conveys commonsense fairness and equality. Those interpretations, however, fail to capture the specific interactional processes that distinguish Relational-Cultural practice from the more conventional usage. In essence, dynamic mutuality describes the flow of power in a relationship. Whether relationships thrive or falter is often a function of how power is distributed and enacted. To clarify the distinctions, I will explain what dynamic mutuality is *not*.

Dynamic Mutuality Is Not Equal Power

First and foremost, dynamic mutuality is marked by shared power rather than equal power. In many societal venues, power differentials are necessary to achieve desired outcomes. Consider the student–teacher relationship. Students enter a learning platform or classroom with specific goals and needs. To accomplish these goals, they must rely upon the availability and expertise of the teacher. Furthermore, the teacher's role is to use her relatively greater power to guide and evaluate students' progress. For the duration of the process, the power differentials inherent in their differing roles are undeniable. In fact, to deny the differences would be to interject an unreality that could ultimately undermine the purpose of the relationship.

Although the teacher–student relationship is not based on equal power, power must be shared in order for the relationship to be most effective. Moreover, the teacher must listen and learn from the student in order to build a strong relational base for the learning. Although it is not within the purview of this book to detail particular pedagogical practices, note that an effective teacher holds dynamic mutuality as an attitudinal stance throughout the relationship with the student. In her book *Connected Teaching: Relationships, Power, and Mattering in Higher Education*, Schwartz (2019) identifies power and vulnerability as the relational assets that the teacher must bring to her work.

While the teacher does not abdicate any roles or responsibilities that accrue to her experience and expertise, she allows herself to grow, stretch, and learn in the presence of her students. Additionally, sensitivity to conflicting social identities and intersectionality is central to pedagogical execution or goal accomplishment. Otherwise, a teacher may use her inherent power like a blunt instrument and crush the student's desire to learn as well as her sense of trust and safety in the relationship.

Dynamic Mutuality Is Not Forced Equality

In the absence of dynamic mutuality, a student may feel trapped inside a power-over dilemma with only lose-lose options. "Lose-lose" is how Harold described his feelings following a meeting with one of his business school professors who was managing an independent study project. Harold was a Haitian American in his late 20s; his professor was a White, widely published, tenured expert in finance. Following the meeting, Harold showed up in my office stunned; actually, seething is a more appropriate descriptor.

What was the cause of Harold's anger? He explained that during the friendly chitchat that was typical of student–professor meetings, the two men started chatting about the threat of a bird flu pandemic that had been in the news. As Harold told it, the professor said to him: "You are going to be okay. The only lethal bird Black men need to worry about is fried chicken." The professor, apparently delighted with his joke, laughed uproariously.

Since Harold needed the professor's expertise and a positive evaluation, neither fight nor flight was an option. So he froze. He sat through the rest of the meeting with a smile stuck on his face while talking through gritted teeth. For that, he was embarrassed. As an adult male who already had achieved significant career accomplishments, not to mention matriculation at an elite business school, he felt helpless and a bit foolish for not knowing how to respond to a comment that he found presumptuous and insulting. The professor, he thought, seemed not to notice the change in his demeanor. Tickled by his sense of humor, he seemed to think he had bonded with Harold.

In other words, similar to what I described in my encounter with Edwin, Harold was simply a prop in the professor's self-narrative. The professor's power in the relationship seemed to make him oblivious to any external realities—including the real presence of the man seated in front of him. Harold could only wonder that if the professor made such a comment to him in his presence, what might he say about him and other Black people in their absence?

DYNAMIC MUTUALITY IN PRACTICE

Consider, by way of dramatic contrast, my son Walker's experience of dynamic mutuality as a 5th-grader in a school system that was approximately 98% White. The 5th Grade Ellis Island Project was a longstanding tradition in the system, intended as a multidisciplinary learning experience. Students were expected to research the stories of their ancestors' experiences coming through Ellis Island. They could dress in period garb and bring any artifacts, photographs, or creative representations to help their classmates visualize the experience.

When Walker told me about the assignment, he was incensed. Given that it was not at all unusual for him to be incensed about 5th-grade homework, I must confess that I didn't fully listen to the first few minutes of his grievance. My ears pricked up when he claimed that teachers should understand that everyone did not come through Ellis Island. Some were trafficked to the United States against their will and others were already here! I was proud and a little taken aback when he then announced that he was going to meet with the principal to explain his viewpoint, because "students should have the right to tell the principal things."

My 5th-grader did meet with the principal, who was able to agree that the assignment needed to be amended and asked how Walker would like to participate. Walker decided to research the customs and the immigration experiences of people from a country that interested him: Egypt. He tackled the project with gusto. By way of epilogue, I never got involved in any of the negotiations. However, when I later spoke with the school superintendent on an entirely different matter, she told me about a 5th-grader whose objections to an assignment prompted the school committee to rethink and change some of their traditional programming and curriculum planning.

This experience perfectly illustrates the core principles of dynamic mutuality. Just as with Harold, there were undeniable and necessary power differentials in the relationships. Each participant had roles and responsibilities to execute. At no point did the teachers and administrators abdicate those responsibilities. Neither was my son excused from participating in what turned out to be a rich, imagination-expanding research experience.

However, more than any data and facts he may have gleaned from the project, my son experienced what Schwartz (2019) calls "intellectual mattering." Intellectual mattering is more than an affirmation of cognitive ability. The experience of mattering to another, whether through intellect or any other capacity, affirms the student's sense of dignity, purpose, and possibility. The student experiences power as the energy of being present and alive because she is participating in shaping her world.

DYNAMIC MUTUALITY IS NOT SYNONYMOUS WITH COMPROMISE

Another common misunderstanding is to equate the practice of dynamic mutuality with compromise. While it is true that compromise is one way of sharing power in relationships, it is definitely not the sine qua non of mutuality. In many instances, compromise consists of bartering away differences—getting as close to an "ouch" point as possible without crossing the line, thus preserving some modicum of self-interest. Mutual empowerment then becomes a byproduct of what is fundamentally a transactional process.

In contrast, dynamic mutuality is a relational process that generates clarity, often by amplifying differences. Dynamic mutuality as a relational practice holds conflict and collaboration as intersecting pathways toward enhanced trust and expanded relational opportunity. Unlike transaction-centered compromise, it decreases the risks of pseudo-harmony, festering mistrust, or lingering obsessions with "winning" the next conflict. Shared power, not power-over, becomes normative.

Again, the 5th Grade Ellis Island assignment illustrates this point. My son approached the conversation with his principal with an energetic commitment to a particular point of view. Whatever the outcome of the exchange, he would not be dissuaded from challenging the premise of the assignment or excused from doing the work. He did not need to dilute the strength of his conviction. In fact, the full force of his conviction helped to bring the issue at hand into sharper focus.

Likely the principal and curriculum planners also held strong viewpoints about the assignment, as it had become a "signature" tradition within the school system. They brought their authority, experience, and expertise to the conversation table. To have done otherwise would have been disingenuous and disempowering for all of the participants in the conversation. They did not abdicate, nor did they hoard power as a zero-sum commodity to be used as a protective barrier against student input. Instead, they claimed their greater power and used it to open new pathways to learning—not just about history, but also to experiencing how it feels to matter in the world.

STRATEGIES OF DISCONNECTION TO RESIST DYNAMIC MUTUALITY

Withdrawal from mutual engagement can take many forms. In some cases, it may look like an assertion of power-over, and in others it may take the form of self-diminution. Whatever the apparent difference, they are strategies of disconnection, disengagement for the purpose of gaining control of the relationship. In my writing and in workshops I have facilitated over the years, I often recall my clinical relationship with a young woman I call Kira (Walker, 2004). I use the story to illustrate how failure to engage emergent realities inhibits personal and professional development, as well as racial healing.

Kira was a 3rd-year college student when I met her, and I was a psychology intern in the campus counseling center. She was concerned because her "bad moods" and bouts of tearfulness led to frequent fights with her boyfriend. Her goal was to "fix herself" so that she would be a better girlfriend. Kira grew up in an affluent suburb, the only daughter in a White, upper-middle-class family. Within three sessions, it was apparent to me that she was also a survivor of sexual abuse. She described the "wild, pot-smoking parties" that her parents hosted nearly every weekend, and casually mentioned that it was not unusual to wake up and find that a strange man had wandered into her room.

As our relationship developed, she started to bring in pictures of her 6-year-old self, one that showed her lip-kissing one of her father's friends. She also began to acknowledge her unease about her sexualized relationship with her father. For example, it was not uncommon for him to stroke both her and her mother and jokingly wonder who "had the nicer ass." Because she had no memory of penile penetration, Kira initially discounted her own discomfort both with her father's behavior and her mother's apparent complicity. Within weeks into therapy, however, she started to feel the pain and name the wounding she experienced in a family that on the surface was "happy and normal." I felt like a very good therapist providing just the care that this wounded young woman needed.

One week, following a particularly tear-drenched session, Kira began describing some of her earlier school experiences. She disclosed that she once went to what she called an "urban" school, but her father made her withdraw because he thought it was "too full of niggers and Mexicans." Armed with a headful of theories about sexual abuse and therapeutic process, I deflected. It was not that I failed to notice the smile on her face when she reported her father's bias; I simply chose to interpret it away. This exchange, I decided, was her attempt to establish a sense of control in our relationship after experiencing such vulnerability the previous week. I chose to frame her inflammatory remarks as her way of regaining a sense of safety through distance.

Instead of engaging her directly, I took the path that felt safer to me: I invited her to talk about the impact of her father's decision on her. Instead of staying present with the racialized dynamics that were emerging in relationship, I hid behind the boundary identity of Caring, Unflappable Therapist. I decided that she was not ready for a conversation about race. In other words, I attempted to put her in her place as the patient who needed my expert ministration. In the therapy room, I had greater status, but in the world outside of that room, Kira was solidly positioned above me in the social hierarchy. Kira promptly dismantled this ploy by saying that she learned "so much more in the better school."

It is not my purpose here to detail all of the clinical nuances of that exchange. In some ways, my interpretations were not wrong, but they were neither right nor useful. Our relationship had offered up a rich opportunity for her and for us to consider what it was like for her to trust her pain with a woman whom she had been trained to regard as inferior. The parallel process is striking. In light of this entrained superiority–inferiority paradigm, I felt compelled not only to shore up my credibility as a fledging therapist, but to prove my worth as a Black woman with brains. In doing so, I missed an opportunity to learn to trust my full humanness—which actually showed up as a gut punch when Kira smilingly talked about "niggers and Mexicans."

Instead of staying present in the relationship with the cognitive-emotional-sensate experience of being an African American woman therapist in the room with a White young female client, I chose to disconnect. Suffice it to say that she was a very bright and sensitive young woman who used provocative language to impact on our relationship. I resisted her influence by trying to inhabit the image of Perfect Therapist, refusing to allow the powers released in our relationship to bring healing to us both.

It is important that I share the epilogue to this story. We met unfailingly on a weekly basis until she graduated. In our final session, Kira wept with gratitude, expressing her affection for me and her appreciation for the help she had received. She went on to confess that when she first saw that she had been assigned a Black therapist, she considered running out of the building. However, her family had trained her to be polite, so she followed me to my office. Once there, she discovered that I not only spoke English well, I said some things that made sense—so she decided to return. Weeks later, I received another long thank-you letter from Kira. This time she mentioned that she had a new therapist, a White male. She went on to share that he had helped her to discover she was a survivor of childhood sexual abuse. I was stunned. Although we had spent many hours talking about the hurtfulness of her father's behaviors, she was apparently unable to internalize those conversations.

I have no doubt that complex racial dynamics were in play in our relationship from beginning to end. The real irony is that however off-putting her "niggers and Mexicans" comment was, Kira was the only one in the room willing to risk naming the divisive realities that we both lived—inside and outside the therapy office. I also have no doubt that my fear of mutual engagement lessened her sense of safety. Upon receiving her thank-you letter, I began to realize how costly my illusion of unilateral control was to our relationship. It was also then that I began to realize that action in relationship literally transforms power, that dynamic mutuality is more than a poetic notion. It is a liberating practice that opens up new possibilities for human connection.

THE SOUND OF ONE HAND CLAPPING AND OTHER CAVEATS

For over a decade a small group of us who were deeply interested in developing relational-cultural theories met for weekly conversations. It was in these meetings that Jean Baker Miller often referred to "the sound of one hand clapping." More than a clever metaphor or Zen koan, the phrase was a reminder that hearkens back to her most fundamental premise: that human growth requires active engagement in relationship. Dynamic mutuality enables deep engagement, and like other relational practices, it is an exercise in the shared power of two hands. It is not an "if-then" algorithm that guarantees a particular desired outcome. Indeed, were that so, it would be at best a negotiation tactic. Her comment was also a humbling reminder that (1) skilled relational practice can devolve into a power-over strategy, and (2) noble intentions do not justify unilateral control.

By definition, dynamic mutuality is a relational stance and process that invites engagement by all participants in a relationship. But sometimes participants do not want to participate. For some people, moving toward shared power is an anxiety-evoking proposition. Whatever the motivation and however it is expressed, resistance to dynamic mutuality is grounded in fear. When addressing racial injustice, whether perpetrated by individuals or reproduced through cultural norms and institutions, the embedded shame and layers of toxicity makes contemplation of mutuality almost unbearable.

During one of my workshops with racial justice activists, I invited participants to call to mind someone with whom they were "at odds" on a particular issue. Following a conversation about the underlying tenets of mutuality, I asked them to notice any concerns that surface. One White woman who could not hold back her tears said that she had worked too long and hard as a social justice activist to allow herself to be "changed" by people whom she saw as the enemies of humanity. To do so would feel like a betrayal of the commitments that define her very being.

Her fear was completely understandable, and her articulation of her concerns helped all of us in the room. First, she was not the only person who felt this fear, and to have it openly expressed released a vibrant energy in the room. Second, my job as a facilitator was to lean into that energy and learn how to share more clearly what certainly has the sound and feel of a paradox: humble confidence. In other words, it is possible—in fact, necessary—to be strongly committed to a conviction while daring to ask: What might I learn from this person and from this situation no matter how different they may appear?

In other instances, resistance to dynamic mutuality is a reaction to external pressures and expectations. I once spoke with a woman about her experience as a lay minister in a church that denies leadership positions to women. In her words: "The only thing worse than being a woman in this church is being a man who loves women." In the history of race relations in the United States, there was a saying that exactly mirrors this sentiment: "The only thing worse than being a nigger is being a nigger lover." Since this notion is rarely openly articulated in 21st-century America, I have to admit my surprise when I recently heard a young person use the term "wigger": a White person who loves "niggers."

The operative function of the slur is the same, whether it is an expression of antebellum mores or 21st-century middle school bullying. It operates as a warning system: Connection with or empathy toward members of a degraded group is to incur taint by association. This power-over tactic functions to keep inequalities in place. To work for social justice is to risk being labeled a "bleeding heart"—never a compliment. A man who is influenced by a woman risks being called "hen-pecked"—a milder form of another moniker that is inappropriate in this text. The warning is clear: To engage in a mutually enhancing relationship with someone who is "less than" is to risk losing social capital, your status in the rank-ordering of human worth.

Finally, there are humans among us who are deeply and fearfully invested in maintaining power-over. These people are invested in personal ascendancy; there is no genuine concern in the subjective experience of others. Awareness and appreciation of the wholeness of another may be experienced as shameful weakness, or worse, defeat. In the worldview of these people, others have only utilitarian value: to take care of their needs, to be the object of discharge of instinctual impulses, or to become a vessel for their transferences and projections (Jordan, 1991). To persist in trying to engage in a mutually empowering relationship under these conditions would be dispiriting and destructive. Again, such futile persistence is also what Miller would call the sound of one hand clapping.

So what does one do instead? Is the only option to retreat behind the hard-line boundaries of a True Self or some other impermeable image of closure and perfection? There is, of course, learning in these situations. Let me take a bit of poetic license here. Another metaphor that I find instructive comes from the song "Go Up, Moses," popularized by Roberta Flack in 1971. The song is an inversion of a spiritual, "Go Down, Moses." Instead of the familiar plaint of Pharaoh, "let my people go," the song exhorts people to "let Pharaoh go." The lyrics say that while Pharaoh doesn't want you, he needs you. Without you, he doesn't exist. The song stands as a challenging reminder that all power, even unjust power, is created and sustained by relationship. It is a "move on" anthem.

"One hand clapping" relationships are hurtful; they may be mind- and spirit-numbing, heart-wounding and body-breaking. What we learn in these relationships is to preserve the integrity and energies that enable us to move on to more liberating relational possibilities. In the chapter that follows, we will explore in fuller detail the anchoring practices that create safety and an expansive imagination of who we can be in the world. Miller (1976) has described the outcome of these mutuality practices as the "fifth good thing" of growth-fostering relationships: increased desire and capacity to be in relationship.

REFLECTIONS

What might the practice of dynamic mutuality mean when it is important to maintain professional boundaries? What cautions should one bear in mind? What benefits might one expect?

Think of someone with whom you're at odds on a particular issue. What are your first thoughts, first concerns, or fears when you hear the word "mutuality"? What concerns do you have about what would be expected of you? How might practicing mutuality affect your work or the values you hold dear to your heart?

CHAPTER 9

Say It Isn't So . . .
and Other Race-Card Games

Let's be clear: The words "playing the race card" are used as an accusation, not an observation. This accusation is typically directed against people who are citing the pernicious effects of racism in their lives. The way this particular card game works is through instant role reversal: Upon hearing that racism may be implicated in a given outcome, the presumed listener turns interlocutor. At that point, the issue disappears, and the speaker is put under scrutiny and not-so-subtly reminded of his (subjugated) place in society. Moreover, once the "race card" is invoked, the linguistic frame is changed. Whatever is at stake in the conversation is framed as nothing more than a political "game." The "race card" accusation suggests, at best, irresponsibility, and at worst, duplicity. The speaker then must defend not only her perspective, but also her integrity. It's a game that no one really wins.

At one time or another, most of us have been left feeling stupefied, wounded, or enraged about how a conversation about race did or did not go. When these feelings arise, it doesn't seem to matter so much how these conversations got started in the first place. Maybe they started with a formal agenda, as when a group or organization decides to have a "difficult conversation" or a "cultural competency" training session. At other times, the conversations seem to happen by ambush: We thought we were talking about something entirely different only to discover that we're in a deeply racialized landscape, either dodging or tripping on land mines. In either case, a common outcome is profound disconnection—from our bodies, our brains, and most blatantly, from the other person in the conversation. Whether out of anxiety, antagonism, avoidance, or likely some mix of the three, the ways we talk about race often solidify the disconnections that shape our sense of who we are in the world.

I recall one such conversation that left me with what felt like an out-of-body experience. My husband and I were having a pleasant after-theater dinner with friends, one of whom was a White male professor. Somehow the topic of race—and inevitably affirmative action—came up in conversation. As each of us was rather freely expressing our differing perspectives, the professor averred that he had no race prejudice, but much preferred working with African students because they were "quicker and smarter" than African American students. He went on to explain that African Americans had likely been tainted through miscegenation. His line of thinking was that the strong Africans killed themselves in the Middle Passage rather than become slaves. Therefore, only the weaker lot, present-day African Americans, survived. In contrast, present-day African immigrants were "undiluted," and thus able to outshine African Americans in the lab and in the classroom any day.

He was completely serious about this evidence-free theory, and I'm pretty sure I completely dissociated. I couldn't believe this conversation was happening in the 21st century, not the 18th. The speaker, a venerated professor at an elite law school, was not only brilliant, he was also a kind-hearted man. A good person/bad person or Model Me/Not Me binary simply could not explain the levels of illogic and racial disdain revealed in his remarks. Yet his comments were devoid of personal insult. So how did after-theater conversation take such a tortuous turn?

IDEOLOGICAL FORCE FIELDS

The answer, I believe, in part is that there exists an ideological force field, part of the culture of racism, that shapes American identity. This culture of racism functions to confer normalcy through messages about place and purpose: who belongs where in American society. Take for example, this little ditty from "Elbow Room" that contemporary author Tim Wise (2011) highlights in his book *White Like Me: Reflections on Race from a Privileged Son.*

> There were plenty of fights
> To win land rights
> But the West was meant to be.
> It was our manifest destiny.

As Wise points out, it is entirely possible to proudly sing that merry tune without ever considering it a celebration of internment, genocide, and theft by conquest. Without such consideration, however, these assaults against humanity are internalized as not only normal, but as a necessary aspect of American "greatness" or patriotism. Put another way, the quintessentially American mythos that every schoolchild learns—for example, that Christopher Columbus was a brave explorer and that western "settlers" are to be admired for their persistence despite having weathered many hardships—normalizes a racial caste system in which groups are "put in their place" by subjugation, annihilation, or simply by rendering them invisible. Persons whose racial identity reflects the dominant side of the caste system need never bother noticing that they exist within a cultural system that valorizes the normalcy or the "rightness" of who they are.

As DiAngelo (2018) points out, White Americans can be deemed qualified to lead major or minor institutions, or graduate from law or teacher education programs without ever having to discuss racism. (She points out that a token "diversity" course, when it exists, is likely to have been hard won and perennially contestable.) Furthermore, the persons on the receiving end of the subjugation exist within the same ideological force field, which solidifies the meaning-making function of the mythos. French existentialist Sartre (1947) describes this function as an "external machine . . . an implacable apparatus" that people must accept, struggle against, submit to or re-invent because it is not within them, they are within it." This perspective partially explains how my professor-friend could be so fervently invalidating without intending personal insult. The ideological force field generates three beliefs that silence change-making conversations about race and its place in our American lives: hyperindividualism, racial innocence, and omniscient entitlement.

Hyperindividualism

It is no surprise that a culture that reifies the Separate Self would also valorize hyperindividualism. This tendency is reflected in the cultural adoration of bootstrappers, people who rise by dint of their own individual effort, presumably without leverage or help from anyone else. The metaphor has cultural appeal, no matter that it flies in the face of logic (pulling oneself up by the bootstraps is a physically impossible feat). In conversations about race, this metaphor reinforces the notion that access to opportunity is equally available to anyone who has the character or initiative to seize it. Therefore, persons or groups who do not succeed in the culture must lack either character or initiative. Not only does hyperindividualism lay blame at the feet of subjugated groups, it completely denies the built-in leverage that benefits dominant group members.

A central theme of Miller's classic work, *Toward a New Psychology of Women* (1976), is that the privileges of the dominant group are interwoven into the fabric of society and are thereby rendered nearly invisible. For example, in contemporary parlance, affirmative action is taken to indicate extra support given to minoritized groups, sometimes by extracting that support from majority groups. Put bluntly, (White) Peter gets robbed to pay (Brown or Black) Paul. This kind of argument is put forth in various venues, from courtrooms to backyard barbecues, and it is based on acceptance of better than–less than racial stratification. Contemporary lawsuits in which a White candidate complains that she (or he) was denied admission to a college because a "less qualified" (usually based on a test score) Black or Brown person "took her place" completely ignores the mix of factors that may be involved in admissions decisions, as well as the salient fact that White candidates who scored lower than she were also admitted. Her sense of her own privilege is invisible when she regards her same-race counter-parts as less likely to have usurped her place.

Furthermore, whatever the outcome of specific lawsuits or decisions, hyperindividualism denies the collective benefits bestowed on members of the racially dominant group. Peggy McIntosh (1988) delineates an array of built-in benefits that include protecting her children from strangers who may not like them, knowing that she will find her race represented in cultur-al media, and relatively trouble-free interactions with persons of authority. Tim Wise (2011) traces such collective privilege to 18th-century naturaliza-tion laws that conferred citizenship only on free White persons, excluding enslaved, indentured, and indigenous nations as well as persons of other ethnicities.

Socially dominant groups *by definition* enjoy built-in collective privi-lege. The privileges are conferred by the social arrangement of "better than" and "less than;" they effectively function to hide the needs, limitations, or vulnerabilities of the dominant group, while making the needs, limitations, and vulnerabilities of the subjugated group hypervisible. Collective or sys-tematic benefit or privilege constructs systematic deprivations. As McIntosh (1988) avers, unearned advantage is interwoven with systematic oppression. However, the cultural ideal of hyperindividualism severs the connection be-tween this racialized arrangement.

Here is a non-race-related example. In the 1990s, much of the con-versation around women's career development would focus on a mommy track. On the face of things, the mommy track seemed a type of corporate beneficence; give women extra support to help them become organizational contributors. What the term obscured was the uneven distribution of the labor of childrearing. Men were expected to move freely about the world—whatever their professional status—without assuming the daily and essen-tial responsibilities of growing a family. That was "women's work," work that often led to closed-off opportunity for women in the business world given their presumed lack of commitment or reliability.

The problem is that hyperindividualism renders collective privilege nearly invisible and undiscussable. For minoritized group members to call it out is to risk their being accused of "playing the race card." For dominant group members to name it and discuss it is to risk ostracism from same-group peers. Furthermore, to deny collective benefit of racial dominance makes it easier to deny complicity in the collective or systemic oppression of racially minoritized groups.

Racial Innocence

One of the more specious ways to stall a conversation about race is to claim racial innocence. It often sounds like this:

- "Nobody in my family ever owned slaves. We worked hard for everything we got."
- "I don't care if a person is black, white, green, or purple. I treat everyone the same way."
- "I don't see color. I just see human beings."

Such comments not only fly in the face of reality, they forestall any opportunity for further growth or exploration. Who can talk about what they pretend not to see?

Take the first comment above. In addition to limiting racism to slave-owning, the speaker delivers a powerful subtextual counterpunch: Lack of hard work, not racism, is the problem. Moreover, asserting oneself as an ahistorical being is an exculpatory claim. In short, it says racism has nothing to do with me. Conversation over. It is worth noting that the claim of innocence can also be made by acknowledging White privilege. As DiAngelo (2018) suggests, comments such as *"I know I'm privileged because I'm White,"* may sound "woke." However, simple acknowledgment falls far short of disrupting complicity with norms and practices that sustain White privilege. In that sense, racial innocence is not too different from saying "Sorry, not sorry."

Racial innocence is commonly asserted through claims of color blindness, not as an optical reality, but as a moral-political stance. In truth, skin color represents politicized groupness in this country that one cannot fail to see or experience. As a polarized political category, color has been grouped historically as White or Black, and though the nomenclature changes over the years to fit the cultural zeitgeist (e.g., colored, Negro, Black and Brown, African American), the political meaning of those groups remains the same. Humans, like other primates, socialize into groups, and always know not only to which groups they belong, but also the meaning of their belonging. Again, DiAngelo (2018) maintains that because groups have no meaning without their comparative opposite, we also know the cultural status that racial group membership confers. However, claims to innocence, likely triggered by racialized anxiety, makes such acknowledgment all but impossible.

Omniscient Entitlement

A third defining feature of the ideological force field is *omniscient entitlement*: the right to define what's rational, what's real, and what's human. The generator of many race-card games, it is as all-encompassing as it sounds and is the source of racialized invalidation. Invalidation, according to Sue et al. (2019) occurs on both micro and macro levels, the former being a primarily interpersonal assault, the latter occurring on more systemic and institutional levels.

An example of micro-invalidation might involve one friend telling another that she is "too sensitive" when the friend reports what she perceives as a racialized slight or discrimination. Gail, for example, told her friend Holly about an in-store cheese vendor who was offering free samples to White shoppers, hoping to encourage a purchase. When she, a dark-skinned Latinx woman approached his counter, he averted his eyes and wandered away—only to return as soon as she left his proximity. Gail's experience of racial discrimination at the eyes of the cheese vendor is then invalidated by her friend's dismissal of its importance. Macro-invalidation is exemplified by school systems that systematically develop and implement policies that result in higher expulsion rates for students of color (U.S. Department of Education Office for Civil Rights, 2018).

Whatever form the invalidation takes, its function is to convey that racism is either nonexistent or inconsequential. Invalidation then may be experienced as a psychological pin-prick (e.g., disbelief about a grocery store encounter) or as a life-altering or life-ending oppression (e.g., imposed school failure or entrapment in the school-to-prison pipeline). This strategy has been repeatedly codified into law; for example, when Supreme Court Justice Roger Taney opined in 1857 that a Black person had no rights that a White person was bound to respect (Kendi, 2016). In other words, White Americans' legal entitlement throughout history to define what is real and what matters has continued to the present day.

While the legal judgments of this 19th-century judge have since been overturned, racialized invalidation persists into the 21st century, when scholars such as Thomas (2008) deem a focus on racial microaggressions as "macrononsense." Similarly and even more recently, Lukianoff and Haidt (2015) asserted that studying racial microaggression is teaching people of color to catastrophize and to have no tolerance for insult. Were these comments not so arrogantly wrongheaded, they would be laughable. Indeed, these pronouncements cannot erase such historical and contemporary realities as Indian removal acts, 246 years of African enslavement, Jim Crow Laws, medical racism, Chinese exclusion laws, Japanese internment, ban on Black jury service, racially biased policing practices, and Black voter suppression. To paraphrase Sue et al. (2019, p. 130), these are the contemporary and historical realities that distinguish racialized aggression from "everyday rudeness" or other radical misfortune. To deny the continuing influence of supremacist ideologies in the 21st century is to invalidate the experiences of all racialized groups. Perhaps it is this dynamic that accounts for the observation that people of color tend to underreport rather than exaggerate reports of racial victimization (Wise, 2008).

To be sure, personalized racial hostilities exist across and within the stratified layers of racial experience. However, it is the ideological force field (i.e., hyperindividualism, racial innocence, and omniscient entitlement) that exacerbates the animus and generates the "race-card games" that derail conversations about race and thwart tentative movement toward cross-racial connection.

In the previous chapter, we discussed dynamic mutuality as a practice that transforms power in relationships. Typically unless there is an impasse or some kind of *felt* inequality, we rarely think of relationships as places where we need concern ourselves with matters of power. But how we practice power in any relationship both reflects and recreates the narratives we call identity. Who listens to whom? Who is open to new learning, and from whom? Who determines not only what is discussable in a relationship, but also when and how it might be discussed? All of these questions address issues of power. We tend to answer them not so much through articulated thought but through habituated practice.

Those habits, in effect, signal our beliefs about who gets to tell the story of who we are as racialized beings and whose story gets silenced. Once a story is silenced, existing power relations remain intact. Therefore, expanding our capacity for understanding and transforming our racialized narratives depends upon our ability to first recognize and next our willingness to resist "silencers" as a key strategy in all race-card games.

THE "SILENCERS"

There are times when we choicefully engage in conversations about race. At other times, we might feel as if we have stumbled into a political minefield—not quite sure how we got there or how to get out. In either instance we might find ourselves feeling silenced—and not always due to our own "word finding" problems. What may be happening is a race-card game in which words are used to silence a conversation—sometimes due to willful aggression and at other times to racialized anxiety. Whatever the case may be, it is important to recognize typical silencing tactics.

One of the common tactics is the Demand for Proof Positive, or what I like to call "Say It Isn't So." Other tactics range from minimization and misdirection to shaming or ad hominem attacks. This list, while not exhaustive, is typical and serves to illustrate commonalities among all silencers. Although the illustrative scenarios below highlight one particular game or strategy, you may notice other "race cards" in play as well. The underlying motivation for silencers is the same: to preserve the racialized hierarchies that protect the narratives of who we are, who we *are not* (read: the Other), and whose story of reality will prevail in contemporary society.

Say It Isn't So

Kerry, the mother of 9-year-old Michael, arranged to meet with Michael's 4th-grade teacher to discuss comments made to Michael by another White teacher. Michael was one of fewer than 25 Black students in his neighborhood school. Most of the other students of color were enrolled in the school through METCO, a state-funded grant program that bussed them from Boston urban neighborhoods to predominantly White suburban districts. Michael, along with other neighborhood kids, was playing after school when the teacher told him to stop playing and get in the bus line to go home. Michael replied that he didn't think he needed to get a bus to go two blocks. Not to be dissuaded by this information about his address, the teacher insisted that he leave the playground, adding that she wasn't going to tolerate "you Boston kids with your attitudes."

When Kerry spoke with Michael's teacher, the teacher explained the pressure on faculty to fill so many roles, one of which was keeping an accurate account and count of the students on the playground. She went on to say that the other teacher was a sweet person whom everybody loved, even though she could be a bit stern and "old school." She insisted that "the teacher didn't have a prejudiced bone in her body" and that perhaps Michael would be better served if he were taught not to be so sensitive.

When Meg went to the pharmacy to pick up some medication, she was relieved to see that the only person ahead of her in line was ending his transaction. However, Meg had to wait another five minutes while the pharmacy clerk and her customer, both White women, laughed and chatted about planned vacations and assorted other personal topics. From Meg's point of view, the women felt comfortable ignoring her because she was Asian. When she tried to explain how insulted she felt to one of her White walking partners, the woman suggested that perhaps they didn't see her. To which Meg responded: "I was in her line of vision—right there at the counter." Her friend then went on to explain that good customer service isn't guaranteed to anyone, and that she shouldn't try to make a "big race deal" out of somebody who may be rude to everyone.

Tim and Joe, two White males, got into a heated argument about the treatment of former NFL quarterback Colin Kaepernick. After Kaepernick was released from his team for kneeling in protest of the extrajudicial violence against Black males by police, other franchises refused to hire the star player, citing fan disapproval of his lack of patriotism (Giglio, 2017; King, 2018). While Tim insisted that the same thing could have happened to a player of any color, Joe pointed out that Black players tend to receive the harshest penalties for infractions of any kind. Tim continued to defend the league, saying that fans want to be entertained, and the owners have a right to protect the value of their brand. He went on to say that the national anthem is part of the game that Kaepernick signed on to play, and if he wanted to make millions of dollars to be political, he should do it on his own time.

These scenarios are undoubtedly filled with ambiguities, as are most real-life situations. The point is not to reach a verdict about whose perspective is correct, but to notice the nearly automatic invalidation. For the sake of convenience, let's call the person who reports the incident the speaker, and let's call the other person the listener (whether any actual listening is happening or not). The speaker may or may not have misinterpreted the reported incident. However, in each case, notice how the "listener" reflexively demands an alternative explanation. The lapse of empathy is glaring when the immediate response to a reported situation is to "Say it isn't so." The message the listener conveys is clear: Safe talk about racism cannot happen in this relationship. Rather than explore or think through her experience, the speaker is admonished to disconnect from her experience: What she feels and thinks is either untrue or inconsequential.

Again, as Miller (1988) noted in *Connections, Disconnections and Violations,* this dynamic is neither uncommon nor inexplicable. In the face of a relational violation, the person holding less power is more likely to disconnect from her own experience. When her presumptive listener—particularly one who is identified with more cultural power—responds with defensiveness, what happens next is exacerbated disconnection. In the above scenarios, the responses of the presumptive listeners consciously or unconsciously protect the hyperindividualism of the racial status quo. In other words, to speak of the consequences of minoritized racial group membership puts one at risk of further disparagement.

The Minimizer

What if evidence of racial violation is not ambiguous—as it is in the scenarios described above—but documented and indisputably codified into law or etched onto placards and concrete signs? In steps The Minimizer.

Consider Lila, an African American woman who was explaining to her White sister-in-law the humiliation her fair-skinned daughter experienced as the only student of color in the 6th grade in a predominantly White charter school. Her daughter (let's call her Caitlin) was basically used as Exhibit "A" when her White social studies teacher was explaining the social and economic structures of slavery. Caitlin, the teacher explained, would likely have been a house servant, and perhaps even a "mistress" and breeder for the owner. Although Lila immediately confronted the teacher and her supervisor, nothing could erase the humiliation her 11-year-old daughter felt. When Lila reported the incident to her White sister-in-law Melanie, she couldn't have been more surprised by her response. "Well, the point of middle school is to learn to handle social conflict. Besides, Caitlin's a pretty girl, and she's popular with her friends. There's no reason to make some big deal out of this."

Imagine the subtext that Lila heard. It was as if her sister-in-law had said "so what" or "who cares." Maria did not characterize Lila's story as a fabrication; however, she did judge it to be a story of no importance—barely worth the telling. Hence, it was the sister-in-law's judgment of the importance of the situation that mattered, not its impact on Lila. This minimizing tactic is a form of entitlement that centers the perspective of White dominance. Let's put it this way: It is hardly surprising when the perpetrator of racial abuse (or those who collectively or indirectly benefit from the abuse) minimizes the effect of the abuse on its targets. It helps to preserve the narrative of racial innocence.

Re-Enter The Boss

One of the more potent silencing tactics in any communication is to seize unilateral control of the terms of conversation. This power-over move may take a variety of forms, to include determining the timing, regulating the tone, and constraining the content of the discourse. Consider the following two scenarios.

Belinda, a Latinx woman in her mid-40s was a newly elected member of the school board in a district where over 60% of the students were 2nd-generation Mexican Americans. In one of the first board meetings, Belinda attempted to point out how little funding existed for arts programs that represented Latinx culture. The board chair issued a stern admonishment: "Our job here is to focus on the education of all children—not to cater to one group's activist agenda."

Aaron, a Haitian American graduate student, complained to his academic dean about an incident that he perceived as racial profiling. A few days earlier, he'd attempted to enter his dormitory housing, but had been stopped and questioned by two campus police officers. After a brief detainment, the officers had explained to Aaron that he "fit the description of a robbery suspect" in a nearby town. The dean, a White male, listened to Aaron's story, and suggested that Aaron take his complaint to Julia, a White woman who was the administrative director of his graduate program. The dean also offered this caution: "Make sure you are polite. It doesn't help you to sound angry."

In addition to spectacular lapses in empathy, both scenarios illustrate how silencing may be used to disempower a speaker who broaches a conversation about a racialized concern. In the first scenario, there is no denying that the board chair may exercise her prerogative to shape the agenda of any given meeting. It is not clear whether Belinda, as a new member of the board, was in violation of any established norms or protocol. If so, the chair might justifiably insist that Belinda follow procedural guidelines. What the chair does, instead, is seize control of language itself. In this context, the descriptor "activist" is no compliment. The chair's word choice is meant to suggest shortsightedness or selfishness on Belinda's part. In this meeting, the linguistic leap from "activist" to "troublemaker" is not long. By defining the agenda to "focus on all children," the board chair seems to have no sense of herself as an activist in support of existing financial (read: power) relations. In other words, "activist" is the label reserved for someone who questions the racial status quo.

In the second scenario, Aaron gets a clear message: How he voices his concerns matters more than the problem itself. In other words, the people with the power to help him address his racial pain must not be discomfited. He is allowed to speak so long as he does so in ways that maintain their entitlement to comfort. Once nudged out of their comfort zone, the deans and directors have no obligation to listen. His reality is rendered invalid.

Ad Hominem Attacks

One of the more potent silencing tactics is shaming. Of course, no one ever has to say, "Shame on you!" Typically, it goes more like this.

Scott, a real estate developer and a longtime member of the small-business council in his town, noted the composition of the community had changed over the past 20 or so years. Given the strong presence and contributions of Korean Americans in the community, he thought it strange that the council had remained all White. He then suggested that the group rethink its outreach and membership practices. His colleague countered his suggestion by saying: "Scott, if I didn't know better I would think you were running for something. Who knew you would turn out to be so politically correct?"

A person unfamiliar with the American cultural context might assume that the two words "politically correct" affirm wisdom and sensitivity. However, they are typically intended as an accusation, not a compliment. The response to Scott's observation carried two clear messages: (1) Your suggestion is unwelcome; and (2) your motivations are suspect. Also implicit in any shaming response is the threat of extrusion, the risk of losing social capital. It introduces the prospect of "not belonging." To use shaming as a silencing tactic is to directly target the neural wiring that supports our human yearning for connection.

It is often noted that language in the American political climate is becoming increasingly coarse (e.g., President Trump's comments about "shithole countries"). However, shaming as a silencing tactic need not be expressed as racial epithets. Just as effective are phrases such as "bleeding heart liberal," "snowflake," or "social justice warrior." All of these terms connote a kind of cognitive and characterological mushiness: someone who cannot be entrusted to protect the narratives of hyperindividualism, meritocracy, innocence, and entitlement.

Shaming, by introducing the prospect of untrustworthiness and not belonging, is a thematic thread that runs through each of these silencing tactics. In fact, none of the illustrations can be parsed for thematic purity. As I mentioned earlier, the scenarios above illustrate typical silencers, not a comprehensive list. For example, the tactic that DiAngelo (2016) calls "channel-switching" (p. 270) is embedded in each of the above scenarios. In general, silencers function to derail conversations, essentially by switching the focus of concern. There are other commonly deployed silencers, such as the use of false equivalences.

Take, for example, the allegation of "reverse racism."

Sometimes, reverse racism is invoked when there is disappointment about a missed promotion or complaints about affirmative action, a practice that, for the record, overwhelmingly benefited White women. Reverse racism may look like this: A White parent complains that his daughter doesn't get enough playing time on the basketball court on a team where the majority players are Black. His daughter may indeed be the victim of racial discrimination. Similarly, a White parent has every right to be distressed and seek redress if her son is being bullied by the Black kids on the street.

In short, racialized meanness, hostility, and discrimination are real and painful across the continuum of racial stratification and may be perpetrated from either end of the "better than"/"less than" divide. These actions and attitudes should never be normalized or accepted as "the way things are." They are not only brutish and destructive, they erode our trust in movement toward more authentic human connection. However, it is a misnomer to equate situational meanness—in the case of a basketball player's court time or neighborhood bullying—with systemic exclusionary practices, inescapable cultural invalidation, and legally sanctioned annihilation.

A FEW MORE WORDS ABOUT RACE-CARD GAMES

At the beginning of this chapter, I mentioned that American identity narratives are shaped largely by an ideological force field—that who we think we are and how we engage or fail to engage each other is often a matter of culturally entrained habit. This ideological force field is something of a wild card in race-card games because it can assume any value required by a particular context or conversation. Because American culture continues to affirm the principles and practices of White supremacy, the deck is loaded to protect the identity narratives of the dominant White culture.

This protection, however, proves fragile. Any disruption to the narratives of entitlement and exceptionalism triggers outrage. The continuum of outrage may range from false equivalences to outright attacks on the character (or sanity) of the person who is naming racialized discrimination. For example: "Racism is the same everywhere. White missionaries experience racial prejudice in Africa." What makes that comment a silencer by false equivalence? White missionaries experiencing racial prejudice in Africa is purely situational. It is rather like the collars that Jane Elliot instructed her students to wear in the controversial Blue Eyed–Brown Eyed exercise (Peters, 1985). At the end of the day, the collars could be removed.

There is yet another twist on race-card games—a reversal of sorts that is generated by the same ideological force field that confers racial dominance. Ensconced atop a racialized hierarchy, members of the dominant group often don't know what they don't know. And what they don't know are the strategies of disconnection that minoritized or subjugated groups learn in order to survive. As Anne Wilson Schaef rather cleverly put it, "people who stand *under* must *understand*" (unpublished proceedings of a lecture, c. 1985).

By way of example, I will close with an old story, one that was told and retold with raucous laughter (and perhaps some embellishment) by my grandparents and great-aunts and -uncles when I was a young child. Someone whom they called Uncle Verdree managed to get a car sometime back in the 1930s or 1940s. He ran a stop sign and was immediately accosted by a White police officer. The excoriation began.

> *Police Officer:* "Boy, what's wrong with you? Didn't you see that stop sign? I ought to lock you up right now. What you niggers need with a car anyway?"
>
> *Uncle Verdree:* "Boss, I don't know what's wrong with me. For sure that is a stop sign. Now let me see: [Slowly, and with exaggeration, calling out the letters] S . . . T . . . O . . . P! Yes sir, Boss. That sure spells stop. S . . . T . . . O . . . "
>
> *(According to the story, this repetitive exchange went on until the officer, possibly first amused at Uncle Verdree's apparent befuddlement, became tired of it.)*
>
> *Police Officer:* "Nigger, get on away from here before I lock you up!"
> *Uncle Verdree:* "Thank you, Boss. You sure a good man."

No doubt the police officer regaled his fellow officers by telling them about the silly old Black man he had let go who barely knew how to read. He could have no idea that the "silly old Black man" knew how to play the race-card game. Knowing the officer's need to feel superior, Uncle Verdree doubled down on dumbness and docility. He conformed to stereotype and made himself the target of derision, thereby turning the game in his favor. The officer left the encounter with his sense of dominance intact, not knowing the "subjugated" side of the racialized narrative. In that narrative the officer was the target of the joke that would provide entertainment for generations of the friends and relatives of the "silly old Black man." No one really wins race-card games.

REFLECTIONS

Although "silencers" may take many forms, the function is invariant. The central underlying function is to suppress the conversation, to make it serve a goal that may be accomplished by deflection (i.e., "channel switching"), minimization, or direct assault. Recall instances of being silenced while trying to engage in a conversation about race. Which of the silencers listed in this chapter did you experience? How did you feel?

Think of responses—questions or statements—that might (a) invite the speaker to question or elaborate on her perspective; (b) signal your willingness to have an authentic conversation on different terms (e.g., change the timing, tone).

CHAPTER 10

Nine Rules for Remaking
the Meaning of Race

Our highest duty is to humanity.

—Madame C. J. Walker

Our cultural legacy has left us with a constricted imagination of who we are and who we can be. Contrary to the aspirational claim that our nation was "conceived in liberty," it was instead built upon the foundational premise of racial stratification. Reflecting on the compromises necessary to unite the federation of states into a nation, in 1858 then Senator Abraham Lincoln observed that without allowing slavery to persist in the Southern states where it was already established, the U. S. Constitution would not have been passed (Delbanco, 2018).

Lincoln was referring to the Three-Fifths Compromise, an agreement that resulted in a mathematical solution to the issues of representation in the legislature and the electoral college. Of the many ironies embedded in this debate, one of the more striking is that it was the slave-owning states that argued for a full accounting of African chattel slaves, thus proposing that the South would hold a numerical majority. However the operational mathematics of this compromise might be calculated, the effect of the Three-Fifths Compromise was the same. Together with the Naturalization Act of 1790, which restricted citizenship to free White people, the compromise consolidated White supremacy and Black inferiority as foundational to a "more perfect union" (Higginbotham, 1978; Kendi, 2016).

Disconnection, based on racialized stratification, has been etched into our cultural DNA. Consequently, the narratives we hold to be true about ourselves (who we think we are) are often deeply conflictual and predicated on distorted relational images of people we perceive to be not only *different*, but "less than" or "better than" ourselves (who we think we are *not*).

Notwithstanding the apparent benefits for some that are seemingly bestowed upon Whiteness in this racial hierarchy, the legacy of stratification, as described by journalist David Brooks (2019), is a corruption that infects the whole society as it traverses down through generations. This legacy has separated us from our hardwired yearning to grow in authentic and meaningful connection to each other. Such authentic, meaningful connections are how we escape the conscriptions of our imagination and enlarge our vision of who we can be in the world.

FIVE GOOD THINGS: CLARITY, CREATIVITY, ZEST, A SENSE OF MATTERING, AND A DESIRE FOR MORE CONNECTION

Psychiatrist Jean Baker Miller is noted for saying that growth-fostering relationships allow us to experience five good things of humanity: clarity, creativity, zest, a sense of mattering, and a desire for more connection (Miller, 1988). Miller's "five good things" are achievable through the anchoring relational practices I've described and illustrated in the preceding chapters: disruptive empathy, mindful authenticity, and dynamic mutuality. Yet for all of our yearning, the legacy from our cultural forebearers often predisposes us to be fearful of authentic cross-racial connection. Indeed, in spite of and perhaps *because of* increased cross-racial contact, we become adept at the strategies of disconnection, often relating to each other on only the most superficial levels. Across social venues, from civic and professional life to more intimate and family relationships, the legacy of racial stratification undermines our desire and capacity for more meaningful connection. We want more; we want to experience the five good things, but desire is not enough. Because our brains and bodies have been imprinted with the legacy of disconnection, simply "being a good person" is not enough. Yet we must try. What's needed are new skills, or rules of engagement, that enable us to learn how to replace disconnection with meaningful connection.

In this chapter, I present nine doable rules of engagement that help us counter the forces that dispose us toward withdrawal and antagonism. I also identify some of the more nuanced strategies of disconnection. Some of these rules of engagement will be "on the spot" practices you can do with your imagination and inside your own body. Others will require ongoing reflection, preferably with the help of others. These rules of engagement will help us move toward a truly "more perfect union" as we transform our inherited relational-cultural narratives and enlarge our imagination of human possibility.

RULE 1:
PAY ATTENTION TO YOUR BODY:
PAUSE, THEN BREATHE YOUR WAY INTO NEW RACIAL NARRATIVES.

We carry the racial narratives that shape our lives in our bodies, and our bodies tell the stories. They are multivoiced stories: our past experiences, our evolving expectations, as well as those stories and expectations that are thrust upon us. The good news here is that the more we pay attention and listen to our bodies, the more clarity we gain about how race is functioning in our lives.

On one hand, there are choiceful interactions, the physical places where we might actually choose to locate our bodies. On the other, there are the more reflexive actions. For example, how do our senses direct us when we're making decisions about safety and comfort? At this point in the broader cultural narrative, it is cliché to mention how the sight of young Black men on the street leads to purse-clutching and street-crossing. However, the truth of the matter is that our racial legacy is such that our brains are imprinted with anxiety. Old embodiments die hard, particularly when they bypass conscious thought.

My first awareness of reflexive embodiment began just a few days after enrolling in a Southern Baptist university, a space that was culturally and emphatically White. As a 17-year-old, I was among one of the first waves of Black students to enroll. All of the Black students had been assigned to one another as roommates; however, on a daily basis in the dormitory hallways we shared laughter, class notes, music, and gossip with our White counterparts. We were all friends—that is until we went outside into more public spaces.

Within a few days my roommate and I noticed that our hallway friends would avert their eyes when we approached them on the sidewalks or cafeteria or any space where our unstructured interactions might be susceptible to social scrutiny. For my roommate and me, the first few days of confusion gave way to laughter at the silly antics of "White girls." Whether out of self-protection, pre-emptive revenge, or just to get a laugh, we would make a game of being the first to look away. Even as teenagers we were aware that our dormmates were under the thrall of old race narratives that prohibited "race mixing." They were too polite to *look* at us and ignore us; *it was the South after all*. Their only option was to refuse to see us. Although my Black friends and I laughed reflexively at the absurdity of the avoidance, we never really thought the situation was humorous. Our laughter was an enactment of the old narratives imprinted on our brains to protect us from racial pain: Don't trust, don't tell the truths, don't feel.

The reality is that now, decades later, the old narratives are still "new." However, when we allow ourselves to become aware of the signals our bodies are sending to ourselves and to others, we can make new choices. It all starts with noticing the tinge of anxiety—whether we are in structured environments such as classrooms or workplaces, a casual environment like a neighborhood barbecue, or someplace as ephemeral as a queue in a coffee shop. Our muscles tighten, and we may start to embody the pre-wired narrative that dictates how we ought to behave. Now is the time to breathe and normalize the anxiety. After all, it didn't start with you. Racialized anxiety doesn't make us bad or unenlightened. It may in fact be a signal that we are waking up to a beckoning toward growth.

A quote often attributed to psychologist Fritz Perls (n.d.) is "Lose your mind and come to your senses." In other words, clarity begins with body awareness, not in the entrained narratives that we may feel compelled to enact. Racialized anxiety may be a physiological reminder that we don't need to enact inherited fear or hostility. Breathing into tightened muscles facilitates relaxation and gives us room to decide how we want to act. Focusing on breathing shifts attention from old relational images that constrict movement and imagination. Then be prepared to experience sparks of self-compassion, curiosity, and maybe even spontaneity.

RULE 2:
BECOME CURIOUS ABOUT THE MULTIPLE RACIAL NARRATIVES IN YOUR HEAD. YOU DON'T HAVE TO BELIEVE OR ACT ON THEM.

Some images we carry fit the narrative of Model Me (our preferred or idealized image) and some fit the Not Me (an image we would be ashamed for others to see). We also carry the images of the Utterly Other (someone whom we consider despicable—irrespective of racial identity). Attachment to these images rules out the possibility of contradiction or multiplicity—yet it is in the contradictions of living that new meanings and new growth occurs.

Consider, for example, the Maryland legislator who in 2019 was censured for calling a majority Black district a "nigger" district (Broadwater & Butler, 2019). Before apologizing, she issued multiple rounds of denial and obfuscation, from lack of recall to admitting to occasionally "taking the Lord's name in vain." Clearly recognizing that using the n-word was politically inexpedient, she persisted in clinging to her Not Me story. Politics aside, suppose she had instead become curious about the multiple and possibly contradictory racial narratives that she carried. Acknowledging multiple narratives would not make her a "bad person." She might instead become a more liberated person, one who is able to participate in her own growth and in the healing of the culture.

I use this example because most of us at some point might have behaved similarly to the legislator or at least have been surprised by the sudden emergence of our Not Me. What is important to recognize is that curiosity opens the possibility of respect, self-compassion, and new choices. In our own lives, curiosity is an antidote to contempt. It allows us to generate questions such as these.

1. What characteristics do I include in my Model Me narrative?
2. What parts of my lived experience do I deny in order to hold on to my Model Me?

3.   What is stoking my impulse to deny: fear? contempt? antagonism?
4.   What do my relationships (personal and cultural) lose when I deny my Not Me experience?

These are the kinds of questions underlying disruptive empathy and mindful authenticity. We become more conscious of legacy narratives that determine who we think we are, and thus more able to subject those narratives to gentle inquiry. The Model Me narrative can be aspirational so long as we don't choke the life out of it by clinging to it too tightly. Likewise, respectful inquiry of the Not Me narrative enables detachment; we become less susceptible to enacting it. This kind of gentle inquiry may also soften the rigid boundaries around the narratives. As we become more detached from the legacy of racialized narratives, our capacity for compassion grows—both for ourselves and for others.

RULE 3:
IF YOU FIND YOURSELF BECOMING HIGHLY REACTIVE IN A RACIALIZED ENCOUNTER, ASK YOURSELF IF SOME DEEP BACKGROUND STORY FROM YOUR OWN LIFE IS GETTING TRIGGERED.

If a group of women are speaking loudly in a public space, do you immediately notice and then associate their volume with their race? If someone cuts you off in traffic are you quick to notice that person's racial identity? Do you find yourself (in spite of best intentions and professed values) feeling judgmental about a mixed-race couple? The fact is nearly all of us have experienced situations in which we have racialized our annoyance.

If you find yourself getting annoyed and hypercritical about a particular behavior by a different-race person, you might ask yourself if there is a personal or a cultural story that accounts for your judgment. What might be the source? If the sight of a mixed-race couple induces agitation, you might remember America's history of anti-miscegenation laws and sexual violence against women and men of color and acknowledge how longlasting and persistent are these negative cultural values. Other times, the trigger may be deeply personal and related to past or current experiences.

I can vividly recall instances when my conversation with a service provider—a salesperson, butcher, or bank teller—was interrupted by a White person coming into the space and interjecting a question of her own. Instead of attributing the behavior to generic, nonspecified rudeness or to an individual's legitimate sense of urgency, my reflexive reaction has been to have a "how dare she!" moment and attribute the behavior to race prejudice.

Some part of that reaction is due to my having spent formative years in a racial apartheid culture, where the needs and convenience of White people always took precedence over the needs of Black people. Mixed with that intergenerational legacy is what the clinical world calls projective identification. I was taught to be polite and considerate, and even as an only child to allow space for others. Consequently, a part of my own growth journey has been to allow myself to literally and metaphorically "take up space." My reflexive reaction might be less due to the other person's behavior than to my cultural and personal biography.

If you notice that you have an automatic, deterministic interpretation to explain an "offending" behavior, you are likely to replay the incident over and over in your imagination. Instead of imprinting your brain with the old interpretations, take a deep breath and try to come up with at least two alternative explanations. Remember that there is no correlation between the quickness of a thought (nor the emotion that accompanies it) and its truth. Not only might this exercise soothe your irritability, it may help you acknowledge the limitations of our inherited stories about ourselves and others.

RULE 4:
ACKNOWLEDGE THE NECESSITY OF GOOD CONFLICT, AND THEN GIVE YOURSELF PERMISSION TO SET THE TERMS OF THE INTERACTION.

In 2012, author Christina Robb and I gave a talk on the politics of racialized relationships as depicted in American fiction. Along with the event moderator, Christina and I participated in a discussion with the audience as they offered reactions, insights, and questions. I thought the 2-hour event went well until I was confronted in the parking lot by a White woman who admonished me for what she called my "uppity, clipped" tone when I responded to her comments, especially when contrasted with what she described as my more relaxed demeanor in responding to people of color in the audience. As I remembered the discussion that had just ensued, this particular woman had made remarks that my co-presenters and I did not fully understand, and we had tried to integrate her comments (i.e., make sense of them) into the larger discussion. That apparently was the wrong tack, and I was being reprimanded for it.

Suddenly I was in the middle of "embodied conflict," the kind that, according to my mentor Jean Baker Miller, was necessary for growth. However, in that moment I knew that the likelihood of a growth-fostering conversation in a parking lot at 10 o'clock at night was nil; I was already exhausted. I also knew that to dismiss her experience out of hand was harmful. I assured the distraught woman that my intention had not been to behave condescendingly and offered to meet with her at another time if she wished to talk through her experience.

This confrontation with a stranger reminded me of a basic guideline for waging good conflict. We are not obligated to talk in the exact moment a conversation erupts or because someone says, "we need to talk." The time, the place, and the neural firings may be such that the conversation may be better if postponed. Many of us in the Western world have a bias toward immediate action; however, immediate action may cause us to jump into situations without having our emotional brain fully engaged with our thinking brain. (*Miller often referred to the value of having clear feeling-thoughts.*) Furthermore, we may think that conversations are "one on one," ignoring the reality that our feeling-thoughts have been shaped by the distortions and violence of racial inequality over the centuries. In setting the terms of the interaction, we are practicing dynamic mutuality—cultivating a relationship process that allows all participants to grow. All participants might ask themselves four questions:

1. What must happen in order for me to consider this time well spent?
2. What personal qualities or experiences can I bring forth to contribute to the flow of interaction?
3. How will I thoughtfully represent at least a portion of what is true for me in this encounter? (In other words, what can this relationship bear at this time?)
4. What tendencies or habits (e.g., avoidance, aggression) must I monitor or hold back if this is to be a growth-fostering encounter?

RULE 5:
RECOGNIZE WHEN "WANTING TO WIN" IS DRIVING THE INTERACTION.

Not surprisingly, our anxiety about racialized interactions can leave us unclear about our goals in, and expectations about, the relationship. Sometimes, we simply want to "win." Winning can mean proving that we are right, making ourselves likeable, unloading our own anxiety, gaining a strategic advantage over the other in some life venue—or effectively vanquishing the other person. What follows are a few common rhetorical moves that signal that wanting to win is driving the conversation.

Silencers

It is not always easy to notice when conflict is devolving into combat, as attempts to win are often disguised as verbal silencers. For example, in academic and training venues, silencers often crop up as excessive intellectualization. I can recall one venue when a participant wanted to have a protracted conversation about whether the word "racialized" (admittedly not common parlance) could be used as a participle.

False Equivalences and Inverse Inferences

One of the more blatant examples of attempts to win conversation is the rapid deployment of false equivalences or inverse inferences. A cultural meme exemplifying both would be to equate Black Lives Matter with Blue Lives Matter or All Lives Matter. A participant attempts to "win" the conversation with inverse inference by suggesting that one issue necessarily implicates an unrelated issue, specifically suggesting that "Black" Lives Matter means that "Blue" lives do not matter. The false equivalency operating in this example is similarly nonsensical. As one training participant put it, "Saying that all lives matter is like refusing to hose a burning house because all houses matter."

Obviously, interacting to "win" disallows any personal vulnerability, any opportunity to learn and grow. Such a mindset affirms the reality that there is more that we "don't see" in any relationship—even one that pops up in a parking lot—than what comes immediately to the surface. Inherited narratives about who we are and what we think we know about the other person(s) largely populate the surface. At those times it is important to ask these three questions.

1. How is what I think I know interfering with my ability to be present and responsive?
2. What am I most afraid of losing if I don't "win" this interaction?
3. How can I speak my truths and allow enough space to experience the other person's humanity?

RULE 6:
WHEN AN INTERACTION APPROACHES AN IMPASSE,
SAY ONE TRUE THING.

My husband Bill is the owner of a contracting business, which brings him into contact with a variety of suppliers, vendors, and customers: people whose values and sensibilities cover the entire political spectrum from what gets called "ultra-conservative" to "extreme leftist." He also publishes a bimonthly newsletter in which he blogs on what he calls "soul care," topics such as contemplative practice, communion with nature, and social justice. One day in a meeting that was presumably about a product issue, one of his suppliers (I'll call him Stu), went "all in," with a tongue lashing about my husband's "off-putting leftist politics." Stu accused him of being not only insensitive to his customer base, but misguided and delusional about how this country really works. He ended his diatribe by announcing that he was unsubscribing to the newsletter and predicting that should Bill continue putting "politics into business," other people would unsubscribe as well.

As was likely intended, Bill heard that announcement as a barely disguised threat. Although his first impulse was to thank him for unsubscribing, he remembered Irene Stiver's advice about authentic responsiveness in difficult conversations (2004). He listened for an opening to add something true and validating to the conversation. He said, "Stu, I can see that you really care about the lessons we can learn from studying our history." To which Stu responded, "Of course. I like history." As Bill recounted the exchange later, he acknowledged all of the things he could have said to give his amygdala some short-term satiation. For example, he might have said "Stu, it's narrow-minded people like you who are causing all the divisiveness in this country right now." (I could certainly imagine all the things I would have wanted to say to Stu.) What proved to be more satisfying, however, was to give himself and Stu a chance to take a verbal breather.

Because of that brief empathic exchange, Stu could (at least for a moment) stop defending his "story" of reality, that is, how he thought about his place in the order of "how America works." Bill was able to experience Stu as a fuller human being, beyond the stance of political antagonist. Months after that encounter, Bill would occasionally mention a Netflix historical documentary to Stu or a book (e.g., Howard Zinn's *A People's History of the United States*) that might offer interesting and novel perspectives on our country's history. Bill's handling of the situation de-escalated what might have become a "lose-lose" conflict. Saying one true thing rather than responding with a more amygdala-satisfying retort allowed the two men to preserve their professional relationship. In addition, this exchange illustrates the impact of disruptive empathy: Both men had to move away from their own self-image to experience the fuller humanity of the other.

The Fallacy of Negative Proof and A Few More Words about "One True Thing"

Our relationships—indeed our culture—are saturated with racialized ambiguities. It is both evidence of our continuing evolution and evidence of how racism works in contemporary times. We are likely to find ourselves flummoxed or shamed into silence if we set out to prove that some disconnection or violation was caused by racism and only racism.

Remember Ken, my student-client in the chapter on mindful authenticity? Not only was he decidedly rude in our initial encounter, he made rather pointed comments about being a "White male" who did not expect others to solve his problems. My brain–whole body interpretation of that remark was and is that Ken was intentionally conveying disrespect for me as an African American woman. However, it would have been absolutely foolhardy and wrongheaded of me to contend that he would not also have behaved that way with a White female or male. That is the problem with trying to prove a negative: You can't. You cannot definitively prove that something would not have happened under different circumstances. Saying "one true thing" about our experience in relationship keeps us off that precarious path of trying to prove a negative. Saying "one true thing" creates spaces where more truths can emerge. Everyone gets to feel protected from contempt. Further, everyone participates in pacing the process of showing up more fully in relationship.

RULE 7:
QUESTION THE NORMS . . . NOTICE WHAT SURPRISES YOU.

In a racialized society, inequality may look completely normal. Imagine sitting in an auditorium in a professional conference in anticipation of a keynote address from the president of an Ivy League university. If an American-born White male steps up to the podium, no one is surprised. We see the person we expect to see. But what if the university president is an American woman from Puerto Rico? Most of us would experience momentary dissonance simply because we would not expect to see her in that role.

Another example: Each year, during the 2 decades in which I worked as a top administrator in an Ivy university, someone (e.g., a student, a visitor) would stop me in the hallway to ask if I could help locate a food item in the cafeteria or fetch something for them. Although I never dressed in the uniform or the chef's gear that the food court employees wore, apparently my brown skin was associated with kitchen service. When I answered their inquiry by saying that I could only help by directing them to someone who actually worked in food service (and pointing to a person who was appropriately dressed), the response was sometimes a look of surprise or embarrassment, and sometimes a hasty exit.

The surprise we feel when our cultural expectations are upended doesn't make us racist; it simply signals the extent to which our brains adapt to cultural norms. After all, culture defines what's normal, what's diverse, what's acceptable, and what's potentially problematic. In his classic 1903 work *The Souls of Black Folk,* historian W. E. B. Du Bois posed the question that continues to mark the experience of those who live on the subjugated side of the racial hierarchy: "How does it feel to be a problem?" Interestingly, the question does not ask how it feels to *have* problems, but how does it feel when one's very being is experienced as problematic in the culture.

I am reminded of an experience (admittedly prosaic in the scheme of awful possibilities) of driving my son 16 miles into Boston to get a haircut because none of the salons in our predominantly White, suburban town was capable of servicing Black clients—not because they were *trying* to be discriminatory, but because the stylists' training did not include cutting the hair of Black folk. As benign as this might seem, this lack of training posed a serious inconvenience to our family. Tired of this biweekly ritual, my son decided to walk into every salon in town to ask if anyone was able to cut his hair. His friend was scandalized: "Walker. You can't ask them that question!" And there you have it. The culture had defined his hair—not the skills deficits of our neighborhood stylists—as problematic.

In Chapter 3, I noted that the dominant group in power-over systems reserves for itself the right to define the terms by which the minoritized group can be known. What this means in practice is that the dominant group may freely off-load any anxiety, shame, weakness, or incapacity onto any member of the "less than" group; that person becomes "the problem." Consider how many features of racialized "power-over" are exemplified in the following scenario. During the course of writing this chapter, my colleague Nina shared another, more recent "hair" experience. Nina, a mixed-race woman with long, voluminous curls, and some of her White girlfriends purchased hair stylings as part of an AIDS charity fundraiser. They went together for their appointments at the participating salon. Upon being seated, it became apparent to Nina that her stylist knew little about how to care for her hair. Worse, she showed no interest in engaging with her to learn. After washing her hair, the stylist instructed Nina to comb her own hair, stating "I don't want to hurt you." As is typical of power-over communication, she framed her desertion of her client as a "service" for the client's own good. With that, the stylist sauntered off to chat with her coworkers, leaving Nina alone in the chair. What had started as a fun day of pampering-for-a-good-cause with friends ended as an experience of isolating humiliation.

From a dominant or power-over perspective, these "hair" examples may seem trivial, or even benign. Additionally, if we are positioned on the dominant side of the racialized (or any cultural) hierarchy, we are less likely to notice the intrinsic inequalities and assumptions. For example, what are the implicit assumptions about who belongs in the neighborhood, or who should be served in the neighborhood? When the owners of the salon opted to participate in the charity event, what assumptions or beliefs did they hold about the charity's supporters? Such implicit assumptions turn into racialized enactments. They are a part of an ideological force field that, though described in Chapter 9 as nonpersonal, translates into acts of personal strategies of disconnection. This ideological force field is the source of many of the deeply held values, beliefs, and behaviors that reveal who we think we are in relation to others—our personal take on what is normal and justifiable in the multiracial world of reality.

We are all likely to be caught by surprise at one time or another, irrespective of our placement in the racialized hierarchy. A typical reaction might be to disconnect, to either deny the surprise or to rationalize it away. A more helpful response would be to acknowledge the surprise and ask questions.

1. What do I have to believe in order to be surprised in this situation?
2. How are my beliefs shaped by how I live in my culture?
3. How seriously do I take these beliefs and what would have to happen for me to consider changing them?

RULE 8:
BE WILLING TO LEARN.

In recent decades we have experienced an upsurge not only in the numbers of, but also in the nature of, cross-racial interactions as our life venues change; our coworkers, social and civic contacts, and even families are becoming less monochromatic and more multiracial. One might expect and hope for a corresponding enhancement of cross-cultural relational competencies. But it's not that easy. Instead, we often hear complaints that these interactions pose a burden of "political correctness." Buried beneath these complaints are often sentimental accounts of the "good old days," when life was simpler because everyone knew their place and cultural norms went unquestioned.

The fact is that cross-racial interactions, especially if they are unfamiliar, are by definition difficult. We are all bound to make verbal missteps and encounter disagreements or interpersonal slights having to do with race. We need to learn how to interact in new ways. Part of what's needed for this learning to occur is what Harvard Business School professor Amy Edmondson calls psychological safety and defines as a climate in which "people feel comfortable sharing concerns and mistakes without fear of embarrassment or retribution" (Edmondson, 2019, p. xvi). In other words, we need to learn how to speak more openly about racial differences and their implications in our everyday lives. We need to be able to say to one another:

"Tell me how I got that wrong."

"What does this mean to you? Please help me understand the importance of this issue to you."

"What can I do to learn more or get better at this?"

"I'm truly sorry; I want to do this better the next time."

In contrast, concerns about the burden of "political correctness" almost certainly reflect incapacity or unwillingness to engage conflict in a manner that results in expanded growth and learning opportunities. Whether mocking the erosion of free speech, or claiming racial innocence (e.g., "I'm not a racist but . . . "), complaints about "political correctness" are often the reactions of someone who feels she or he has a right to disregard the impact of their speech on others. However, feeling comfortable enough to speak up and share concerns in a psychologically safe climate does not include disrespecting others.

Edmondson points out that we go to great lengths, especially in environments where psychological safety is low, to avoid being seen as "ignorant, incompetent, or disruptive" (2019, p. 5). This avoidance results in feeling too fearful to speak up or ask questions that are integral to the learning process. In much the same way, we will go to great lengths to avoid being seen by others as uncaring, culturally obtuse, or racist. Look a little deeper and lurking beneath strident objections to "political correctness" is likely to be a quagmire of unpleasant emotions: resentment, guilt, or shame about verbal misdeeds—those that the speaker might have committed in the past as well as those to which she feels entitled in the future.

The plain fact is that the only way to learn about the cultural joys and pains of the other is to interact across cultures. We all inherited the principles and practices of White supremacy as part of our cultural DNA, yet our lives are not determined by that legacy. We break the deterministic hold on our futures when we are able to, as much and as often as possible, cultivate the psychologically safe places that enable us to embrace the vulnerability of uncertainty and mistakes.

Imagine this. The new studies in biological sciences reveal that whether or not a gene is expressed is largely determined by environmental and lifestyle choices (Mate, 2003; van der Kolk, 2014). Imagine how much more relevant this insight might prove for the ways we structure our relationships with others. To build a just, compassionate, and civilizing culture, we must feel psychologically safe enough to be able to listen, learn, and be changed by each other. Our narratives about "who we are" are works in progress; we are each other's coauthors.

RULE 9:
KNOW WHEN TO WALK AWAY.

In American culture, we pride ourselves on winning—bringing a job or project to our desired outcome. It's not surprising that we might apply that same ethos to our relationships—our interactions with each other. In the case of conflict or simple disagreement (and rarely is racialized disagreement simple), our desired outcome may be converting the other person to our point of view. Rule 9 is this: We have neither the responsibility nor the right to change another person's mind. We do have a right to voice our emergent truths with clarity and conviction. We do have a right to be treated with respect, as well as a responsibility to treat others respectfully. We have a right to protect ourselves from harm; we have absolutely no responsibility to subject ourselves to a haranguing, soul-damaging interaction with another person—short-term or long-term. In other words, we should know when to walk away—when to preserve our energy and our spirits for a new day.

REFLECTIONS

Select one of the "rules of engagement" that resonates with your experience of a positive cross-racial relationship. What are you learning about your own emerging truths in that relationship?

Select one of the rules that you might find challenging. How might any of the relational practices—disruptive empathy, mindful authenticity, or dynamic mutuality—be helpful to you? How do you know when it is appropriate to walk away? Under what circumstances is "walking away" avoidance? Under what circumstances does walking away preserve capacity for continuing growth in connection with others?

CHAPTER 11

An Enlarged Vision
of Human Possibility

> As other perceptions arise . . . the total vision of human possibilities enlarges
> and is transformed.
>
> —Jean Baker Miller

Growing up in the South, I often participated in a bonding ritual with friends and family that serves as an apt metaphor. It was called "walking a piece of the way" (Walker, 2004). After walking to visit a cousin or aunt's home, the guests would be joined by their host, who would often accompany her visitors "a piece of the way" back to their own home. Sometimes this elaborate (and admittedly circuitous) ritual would involve a few back-and-forths. However, there was never any confusion about where "home" was. Friends or cousins or sisters would take their leave, holding the visit and each other in their hearts.

Our most problematic, intractable, and potentially harmful interactions may be framed in the same way. You might have experienced or recall hearing about the many fractious conversations that happened around the Thanksgiving table after the 2016 U.S. presidential election. Brothers and sisters, uncles and in-laws who found themselves on opposite sides of the political divide declared each other morally, mentally, and irreparably "flawed." In some instances, reaching "common ground" seemed not only impossible, but also repugnant! Rule 9 reminds us that inability to reach common ground with another person or change her mind is not failure. Nor is it the end of our concern for one another as human beings. We might continue to hold that person in our hearts, if not at our dinner table. Perhaps our stories—our sense of who we are—may be enhanced just by "walking a piece of the way" in each other's lives. In this sense, to walk a piece of the way is to risk disruption of narratives that anchor our sense of who we are and who we must be in the world.

Not surprisingly, narratives shaped by an intergenerational legacy of racial stratification limit our imagination of human possibility, leaving us susceptible to anxiety, self-doubt, and animosity. To mitigate this racialized stress, we may intentionally or reflexively create large comfort zones with few, if any, permeable boundaries. We then populate these zones (e.g., book clubs, workplaces, neighborhoods) with people "like us": those we presume to share our values, beliefs, and relational habits. Everybody needs a comfort zone, but to confine oneself to a default community of sameness forecloses opportunities for new learning and growth. Creating echo chambers makes it unlikely that we will ever hear anything new.

In order to move toward new relational possibilities, we must intentionally cultivate communities of differentiated allies. We need allies, first, because new growth is an inherently relational process. Second, differentiation introduces the potential for growth-fostering conflict. To define an ally, it helps to answer the questions: *What would an ally not do? What would an ally do?*

What allies do *not* do: First, allies do not retreat from conflict. Second, allies do not rescue each other from challenge or conflict. Third, allies do not presume to *speak for* another person, thereby intimating that the person is powerless to speak for herself. Sometimes allies inhabit more structural or social power, but not always. Put simply, being an ally is not a uni-dimensional performance. Instead, to be an ally is to participate in an evolving process of standing with, stimulating, and supporting another person who is confronting what I might call a "soul challenge"—a violation that threatens her sense of being and mattering in the world. This challenge need not be integral to the ally's lived experience but may be core to her sense of justice.

So what would an ally do? Let me answer this question by sharing my experience from a consultation project with a school district in the Midwest. Over the course of the project, I worked extensively with Dolores, a middle school curriculum director and one of two African American directors in the school district. She reported that for many years the middle school curriculum included an interdisciplinary project to help students understand the importance of the *Brown v. Board of Education* Supreme Court ruling, which declared public school segregation unconstitutional. To reinforce the traditional classroom activities, the social studies and English teachers employed a regional acting troupe to present a re-enactment of the Little Rock Nine's attempt to enroll in a segregated high school in 1957. As Dolores described it, this curriculum component allowed the 11- to 13-year-old students to deepen their thinking by trying on different roles and perspectives. As far as Dolores knew, everyone considered the activity valuable, not only because it reinforced core curriculum objectives, but also because the students seemed to enjoy it.

Imagine her surprise when a White math curriculum director stood up in an end-of-year evaluation meeting to say that the activity should be dropped because it was a "downer" for everyone. Dolores was the only African American in the meeting, and she was stunned into silence. She was confident, however, that one of her White colleagues would challenge this perspective. When no one else spoke, either to agree or disagree with the math teacher, Dolores exited the meeting. The next day, one of the English teachers, a White woman whom Dolores had considered an ally, telephoned to tell her how awful she felt. When Dolores asked why she didn't speak up in the meeting, she responded that she didn't know what to say. "Besides," she countered, "no one takes this guy too seriously." She then went on to explain to Dolores that she thought that someone else could better articulate an opposing viewpoint. *This is not what allies do.*

A few days later, Dolores met with the middle school principal who facilitated the meeting. Upon hearing her disappointment about how the matter was managed, he suggested that she go and have a talk with the math teacher. While that might seem to be a reasonable suggestion, Dolores objected on three grounds: (1) She had no desire to "educate" a public school teacher on the importance of the issue; (2) she didn't consider the conflicting views to be a personal issue between herself and the math teacher; and (3) the math teacher did nothing wrong by responding to the principal's request for feedback about the Little Rock Nine performance.

When the school reopened after the summer break, Dolores continued to feel distanced from her putative allies, but no one made further mention of the end-of-year conflict. Once again, she was surprised when a social studies instructor casually mentioned that a trip to a gospel and blues venue was slated to replace the acting troupe's performance. In other words, a committee that excluded Dolores opted to substitute entertainment for engagement. This time, Dolores went into action. She arranged meetings with each of the teachers and asked what they knew about the decision process, whether they opposed or supported it, and if they were willing to join her in a quest for more information. This time, she and three other educators— two White teachers and an African American school counselor—became allies who formulated a list of questions to be discussed in a meeting with the principal.

1. How and when was the decision made?
2. How were the participants in the decision process selected?
3. On what basis were potential participants excluded from the decision process?
4. In what ways did the selected activity support the core curriculum requirement to address issues of school desegregation?

You notice that none of these questions is designed to force a reversal of the decision. Not one of the questions is an attack on any individual. However, they acted as allies when they came together to address a larger issue: that of cultivating a school culture of inclusivity, respect, and a social vision of equality. They came together and were able to devise an action plan to encourage clarity, agency, and an environment that fosters relational capacity.

Allies do not have to know "the answer." They don't have to share the same experiences or perspectives. What they share is a commitment to stay in connection with each other in ways that allow their multiple truths to emerge, as well as a commitment to grow together, and perhaps to be changed by each other.

ABOUT ALLIES AND RACIAL PRIVILEGE

There are times when a person with greater social privilege and power in a racialized hierarchy might be able to use that privilege in support of racial justice and equity. As journalist Renee Graham suggested in a 2018 *Boston Globe* opinion piece, to deny or simply bemoan White privilege may be to fortify the boundaries of a comfort zone. "If I had white privilege," she wrote, "I don't think I would be ashamed of it. I would use it to expose injustice and make things work better." Using racial privilege to expose and rectify racial inequality will land even the socially entitled outside of their comfort zone. And as one might glean from the book *The Education of a WASP* (Stalvey, 1970), social validation is a hard habit to break. White allies need non-White allies to take the intentional steps that convert comfort zones into safety zones. Those allies necessarily include people who may not look and think alike all the time. In fact, allies occasionally annoy each other. What makes them allies is the commitment to transforming life-constricting narratives of identity into more liberating narratives of human possibility.

REMAKING THE MEANING OF RACE IN OUR LIVES: A FEW FINAL WORDS

On a rainy November morning, a full 20 years after my son had been searched in the middle of a supermarket, I sat in a high school auditorium where Dr. Beverly Daniels Tatum (2018) was leading a seminar with over 400 educators. She began her presentation with a short reflection exercise; each of us was asked to complete the sentence "I remember_____." The reflection invited us all to remember our first awareness of race, racial difference, and racial mattering. Furthermore, we were urged to consider how and with whom that awareness was processed. Exercises such as these are valuable because they help us to re-process (or process for the first time) our stories of racial origin: the stories that shape who we think we are.

Let us return to Chapter 1: The "It" Without A Name. The denials, explanations, and recriminations subsequent to my son's backpack being searched in the middle of a supermarket had one consistent theme: "It" was not about race. Although the experience was humiliating, he knew that what was happening *to* him was not *about* him. He was partially inured from the trauma by his growing knowledge of how race works in American culture.

My own origin story was much different; it happened decades earlier when I was a 4-year-old living in the racial apartheid culture of the American South. My great-grandmother Mary was taking me on a bus ride to downtown Augusta to do some shopping. The excursion inevitably meant wide boulevards, gleaming storefronts, and an ice cream cone. So taken was I with the excitement of it all that I plopped down on the first empty seat on the bus while my great-grandmother deposited our dimes for the ride. Immediately there was nervous laughter on the bus—a bus with only Black women on it at that moment (everyone but the driver), who were probably on their way to shop downtown or headed to domestic jobs.

My reverie about gleaming storefronts and ice cream cones was broken when my great-grandmother roughly snatched me off the seat and steered me to the rear of the bus where the other women sat. I heard someone whisper, "That poor child don't know that's where White people sit." Well, that was true. Not only did I not know where White people sit, I also didn't know what White people were. At that moment, however, I did learn that I wasn't "White people," and that somehow meant that I wasn't good enough. What was worse, I was the only one on the bus who didn't know that fact of life. I remember feeling truly stupid. Unlike my son, as a 4-year old I believed that the "It" was a problem within me.

We all have origin stories about race and our awareness of how race functions in our lives. We have inherited a legacy of narratives, codified by law and corroborated by social norms, grounded in the insistence that race matters as a signifier of our inherent human worth. To extrapolate from a classic work by Margaret Wheatley (2002), race matters when one group of people has the power to enforce the decision that they are more human than another group of people. In spite of shifts in ethnic and phenotypic constellations, racialized distortions of power have persisted through the centuries based on the ideological premise of White supremacy and Black inferiority. However one is positioned in the racial hierarchy, no one is left completely unscathed by this relational dynamic. We bear the scars of the legacy narratives that inscribe who we are and prescribe who we must be. Exacerbating this racialized dynamic is our American mythos of hyperindividualism, which breeds fear of loss: loss of material resources, of social status, and of ontological meaning. It generates a perception of scarcity and a need for a marginalized "Other," a lesser being whose existence justifies exclusion and suppression by whatever means necessary.

We do have the power and the responsibility to create new narratives and norms of possibility, ways of being that are consistent with our biological impulse for authentic connection with each other. When I first visualized this book in conversations with Jean Baker Miller and Judith Jordan,

I wanted to call it *Revolutionary Hope*. In our conversations, we discussed racism as a traumatizing relational dynamic, enacted through distorted and malignant power arrangements. It is a disorder that metastasizes not only through our laws and cultural norms, but through our everyday interactions.

When Getting Along Is Not Enough is an invitation and a portal to those new possibilities. The scholars, researchers, and practitioners of Relational-Cultural Theory have demonstrated that we come into being through action and presence in relationship. As voiced by many of Jean Baker Miller's students and patients, this is the guiding ethos—the way of knowing and being that changes everything (Robb, 2006). It is not through hyperindependence and separation from each other that we become more fully and authentically into being, but through cultivating capacity for responsiveness in relationship. Narratives that valorize hyperindividualism make us susceptible to illusions of separation, as well as to seemingly intractable practices of disconnection. They not only leave us unable to repair the uninterrupted legacy of racism that disrupts our life in the 21st century, they foreshorten our imagination of who we can become. We are left entrapped in binary frameworks of racially woke versus racially obtuse, good versus bad, and Us versus Them. So long as we cling to these constrictive frameworks, we can't breathe life into new ways of being.

The anchoring practices of disruptive empathy, mindful authenticity, and dynamic mutuality help us to navigate the complexities, ambiguities, and contradictions of our racialized lives in 21st-century American life. There are no shortcuts; there is no absolution through adjacency. In other words, mere cross-racial contact is not enough. Having a best friend or a family member of a different race provides no immunity against the ravaging of a racially divided culture. In fact, we have seen over the centuries that mere contact can make us ever more inventive in our strategies of disconnection. (We might remember that enslaved people were in unremitting contact with their owners.)

To be sure, when we begin facing each other with the pain and the fears, with the complexities and contradictions of our living stories, we will likely be plunged into life-giving conflict. Rather than nursing and rehearsing our old fear-based, unidimensional stories, we can use this kind of conflict to move us into the multidimensional voices of our emergent experience in relationship. There is a popular aphorism that claims we get to know each other by walking a mile in each other's shoes. What is typically left unsaid is that walking in another's shoes means we must be willing to shed our own. Clearly, shedding our own metaphorical shoes swiftly places us outside of our comfort zones. However, we must be willing to try on new perspectives in order to draw out our human potential for healing, that is, to create robust neural pathways that enable new ways of making meaning of our lives.

I offer *When Getting Along Is Not Enough* as an invitation to reclaim that yearning and as a guidebook to new possibilities. As the ideas and practices of Relational-Cultural Theory were developing, Jean Baker Miller urged us to call our writings Works in Progress. There is a no more poignant reminder that we are beings in progress. We have the power and the duty to call each other into fuller experiencing of our shared humanity.

References

Adams, R. (2010). *MUD and the five good things*. Unpublished transcript. Jean Baker Miller Training Institute.

Adichie, C. N. (2009, July). *The danger of a single story*. Retrieved from www.ted.com/talks/chimamanda_adichie_the_danger_of_a_single_story

Anderson, E. (2015). The white space. *Sociology of Race and Ethnicity, 1*(1), 10–21.

Associated Press (1990, November 2). Police, town officials apologize to Boston Celtics player. *AP News.* Retrieved from www.apnews.com/b9fc5f80815bb1e8579c72fc2c8a7327

Associated Press. (1991, October 24). BASEBALL; Carter defends use of the chop. *New York Times.* Retrieved from www.nytimes.com/1991/10/24/sports/baseball-carter-defends-use-of-the-chop.html

Associated Press. (1997, April 22). Tiger Woods describes himself as "Cablinasian." *AP News.* Retrieved from www.apnews.com/458b7710858579281e0f1b73be0da618

Banaji, M. R., & Greenwald, A. G. (2013). *Blindspot: Hidden biases of good people.* New York, NY: Delacorte Press.

Banks, A., & Hirschman, L. A. (2015). *Four ways to click: Rewire your brain for stronger, more rewarding relationships.* New York, NY: Penguin Group.

Benedictus, L. (2013, July 15). How Skittles became a symbol of Trayvon Martin's innocence. *The Guardian.* Retrieved from www.theguardian.com/world/shortcuts/2013/jul/15/skittles-trayvon-martin-zimmerman-acquittal

Bivens, D. K. (1995). What is internalized racism? Retrieved from www.racialequitytools.org/resourcefiles/What_is_Internalized_Racism.pdf

Bonilla-Silva, E. (2014). *Racism without racists: Color-blind racism and the persistence of racial inequality in America* (4th ed.). Lanham, MD: Rowman & Littlefield.

Broadwater, L., & Butler, E. (2019, February 26). Maryland delegate's use of racial slur draws outrage from lawmakers, civil rights advocates. *Baltimore Sun.* Retrieved from www.baltimoresun.com/news/maryland/politics/bs-md-delegate-apology-20190226-story.html

Brodkin, K. (1996). Race and gender in the construction of class. *Science & Society, 60*(4), 471–477.

Brodkin, K. (1998). *How Jews became white folks and what that says about race in America.* New Brunswick, NJ: Rutgers University Press.

Brooks, D. (2019, March 7). The case for reparations: A slow convert to the cause. *New York Times.* Retrieved from www.nytimes.com/2019/03/07/opinion/case-for-reparations.html

Brown, D. L. (2019, April 5). Ann Atwater's amazing rise from advocate for the poor to "Best of Enemies" stardom. *Washington Post*. Retrieved from www.washingtonpost.com/history/2019/04/05/ann-atwaters-amazing-rise-poverty-teen-pregnancy-best-enemies-stardom/

Bruteau, B. (2005). *The holy Thursday revolution*. Maryknoll, NY: Orbis Books.

Burns, R. A. (2010, June 15). Sweatt, Heman Marion. *Handbook of Texas Online, Texas State Historical Association*. Retrieved from tshaonline.org/handbook/online/articles/fsw23

Carkhuff, R. R. (2000). *The art of helping in the 21st century* (8th ed.). Amherst, MA: Human Resources Development.

Cartwright, S. A. (1967). The diseases and peculiarities of the Negro race. *De Bow's Review of the Southern and Western States, 11*. New York, NY: AMS Press. (Original work published 1851)

Cole, E. R. (2009). Intersectionality and research in psychology. *American Psychologist, 64*(3), 170–180.

Collins, P. H. (2000). *Black feminist thought: Knowledge, consciousness, and the politics of empowerment*. New York, NY: Routledge.

Copeland, P. (2018, November). Panel Discussion: "The Impact of Everyday Racism." In L. Parker, Jr. (Moderator), *Race, Racism and Mental Health*. Conference conducted at the Charles Hamilton Houston Institute for Race & Justice at Harvard Law School, Cambridge, MA.

Cross, W. E., Jr. (1991). *Shades of black: Diversity in African-American identity*. Philadelphia, PA: Temple University Press.

Davidson, O. G. (1996). *The best of enemies: Race and redemption in the New South*. New York, NY: Scribner.

DeAngelis, T. (2009, February). Unmasking "racial micro aggressions." *American Psychological Association Monitor on Psychology, 40*(2), 42.

Delbanco, A. (2018). *The war before the war: Fugitive slaves and the struggle for America's soul from the Revolution to the Civil War*. New York, NY: Penguin Press.

DiAngelo, R. (2016). *What does it mean to be White: Developing White racial literacy*. New York, NY: Peter Lang.

DiAngelo, R. (2018). *White fragility: Why it's so hard for White people to talk about racism*. Boston, MA: Beacon Press.

Dias, E., Eligon, J., & Oppel, R. A., Jr. (2018, April 17). Philadelphia Starbucks arrests, outrageous to some, are everyday life for others. *New York Times*. Retrieved from www.nytimes.com/2018/04/17/us/starbucks-arrest-philadelphia.html

Doane, A. W., & Bonilla-Silva, E. (Eds.). (2003). *White out: The continuing significance of racism* (1st Ed.). New York, NY: Routledge.

Dovidio, J. F., & Gaertner, S. L. (Eds.). (1986). *Prejudice, discrimination, and racism*. San Diego, CA: Academic Press.

D'Souza, D. (2012). *Obama's America: Unmaking the American dream*. Washington, DC: Regnery Publishing.

D'Souza, D. (2017). *The big lie: Exposing the Nazi roots of the American left*. Washington, DC: Regnery Publishing.

D'Souza, D. (2018). *Death of a nation: Plantation politics and the making of the Democratic party*. New York, NY: St. Martin's Press.

Du Bois, W. E. B. (2005). *The souls of black folk*. New York, NY: Barnes & Noble Classics. (Original work published in 1903)

Edmondson, A. C. (2019). *The fearless organization: Creating psychological safety in the workplace for learning, innovation, and growth*. Hoboken, NJ: John Wiley & Sons.

Eisenberger, N. I., Lieberman, M. D., & Williams, K. D. (2003). Does rejection hurt? An fMRI study of social exclusion. *Science, 302*, 290–292.

Eligon, J. (2018, November 13). Hate crimes increase for the third consecutive year, F.B.I. reports. *New York Times*. Retrieved from www.nytimes.com/2018/11/13/us /hate-crimes-fbi-2017.html

Fisher, L. (2014, January 21). 5 white celebrities whose use of n-word backfired. *ABC News*. Retrieved from abcnews.go.com/Entertainment/white-celebrities -word-backfired/story?id=21601921

Follett, M. P. (1951). *Creative experience*. Gloucester, MA: Peter Smith Publishing.

Fonda, J. (2016, March 23). *My convoluted journey to feminism*. Retrieved from www.lennyletter.com/story/jane-fonda-my-convoluted-journey-to-feminism

Frank, A. W. (2010). *Letting stories breathe: A socio-narratology*. Chicago, IL: University of Chicago Press.

Freud, A. (1937). *The ego and the mechanisms of defence*. New York, NY: Routledge.

Freud, S. (1961). Female sexuality. In J. Strachey (Ed.), *The standard edition of the complete psychological works of Sigmund Freud: Vol. 21. The future of an illusion, civilization and its discontents, and other works* (pp. 223–246). London, England: Hogarth Press.

Gaertner, S. L., & Dovidio, J. F. (1986). The aversive form of racism. In J. F. Dovidio & S. L. Gaertner (Eds.), *Prejudice, discrimination, and racism* (pp. 61–89). San Diego, CA: Academic Press.

Gaertner, S. L., Dovidio, J. F., & Johnson, G. (1982). Race of victim, nonresponsive bystanders, and helping behavior. *The Journal of Social Psychology, 117*(1), 69–77.

Gibson, L. (2018, November–December). The bits the Bible left out: Karen King plumbs early Christianity. *Harvard Magazine, 121*(2), 40–45.

Giglio, J. (2017, August 24). NFL executives explain why Colin Kaepernick is still unemployed. *NJ.com*. Retrieved from www.nj.com/sports/2017/08/nfl_execu-tives_explain_why_colin_kaepernick_is_sti.html

Goleman, D. (1995). *Emotional intelligence: Why it can matter more than IQ*. New York, NY: Bantam Books.

Graham, R. (2018, April 24). Use your white privilege to fight racism. *The Boston Globe*. Retrieved from www.bostonglobe.com/opinion/2018/04/24/use-your-white-privilege-fight-racism/l3kE21EFsMpTF6uboe72pl/story.html

Haynes, S. R. (2002). *Noah's curse: The biblical justification of American slavery*. New York, NY: Oxford University Press.

Helms, J. E. (Ed.). (1990). *Black and white racial identity: Theory, research, and practice*. New York, NY: Greenwood Press.

Helms, J. E., & Carter, R. T. (1990). Development of white racial identity inventory. In J. E. Helms (Ed.), *Black and white racial identity: Theory, research, and practice* (pp. 67–80). New York, NY: Greenwood Press.

Herrnstein, R. J., & Murray, C. (1994). *The bell curve: Intelligence and class structure in American life*. New York, NY: Free Press.

Higginbotham, A. L. (1978). *In the matter of color: Race and the American legal process: The colonial period.* New York, NY: Oxford University Press.

Hillman, J. (1964). *Suicide and the soul.* New York, NY: Harper & Row.

Holvino, E. (2010). Intersections: The simultaneity of race, gender and class in organization studies. *Gender, Work and Organization, 17*(3), 248–277.

Ignatiev, N. (1995). *How the Irish became white.* New York, NY: Routledge.

Itzkoff, D. (2017, June 3). Bill Maher apologizes for use of racial slur on "Real Time." *The New York Times.* Retrieved from www.nytimes.com/2017/06/03/arts/television/bill-maher-n-word.html

Jacoby, J. (2018, August 6). At Smith College, the racist incident that wasn't. *The Boston Globe.* Retrieved from www.bostonglobe.com/opinion/2018/08/06/smith-college-racist-incident-that-wasn/DqB70T11oFZ4LHm6j5z6IM/story.html

Jensen, A. R. (1969). How much can we boost IQ and scholastic achievement? *Harvard Educational Review, 39*(1), 1–123.

Jonas, M. (2012, September 18). Romney's "givers and takers" moment. *CommonWealth Magazine.* Retrieved from commonwealthmagazine.org/politics/001-romneys-givers-and-takers-moment/

Jones, J. M. (1997). *Prejudice and racism* (2nd ed.). New York, NY: McGraw-Hill.

Jordan, J. V. (1984). Empathy and self boundaries. *Work in Progress, No. 16.* Wellesley, MA: Stone Center Working Paper Series.

Jordan, J. V. (1990). Courage in connection: Conflict, compassion and creativity. *Work in Progress, No. 45.* Wellesley, MA: Stone Center Working Paper Series.

Jordan, J. V. (1991). The meaning of mutuality. In J. V. Jordan, A. G. Kaplan, J. B. Miller, I. P. Stiver, & J. L. Surrey (Eds.), *Women's growth in connection* (pp. 81–96). New York, NY: Guilford Press.

Jordan, J. V. (2002). A relational-cultural perspective in therapy. In F. Kazlow (Ed.), *Comprehensive handbook of psychotherapy: Vol. 3. Interpersonal, humanistic, existential* (pp. 233–254). New York, NY: John Wiley & Sons.

Jordan, J. V. (2004). Therapist authenticity. In J. Jordan, M. Walker, & L. Hartling (Eds.), *The complexity of connection: Writings from the Stone Center's Jean Baker Miller Training Institute* (pp. 67–72). New York, NY: Guilford Press.

Jordan, J. V. (2010). *Relational-Cultural Therapy.* Washington, DC: American Psychological Association.

Jordan, J. V. (2017). *Relational-Cultural Therapy* (2nd ed.). Washington, DC: American Psychological Association.

Jordan, J. V., Kaplan, A. P., Miller, J. B., Stiver, I. P., & Surrey, J. L. (1991). *Women's growth in connection.* New York, NY: Guilford Press.

Jordan, J., Walker, M., & Hartling, L. (Eds.). (2004). *The complexity of connection: Writings from the Stone Center's Jean Baker Miller Training Institute.* New York, NY: Guilford Press.

Kanoute, O. (2018, July 31). Facebook post. Retrieved from www.facebook.com/oumou.kan/posts/2079194112329065

Kendi, I. X. (2016). *Stamped from the beginning, The definitive history of racist ideas in America.* New York, NY: Nation Books.

King, M. L., Jr. (1960, April 17). *Interview on "Meet the Press."* Interview by N. Brooks in Spivak, L. E. Meet the Press [Television broadcast transcript]. Retrieved from kinginstitute.stanford.edu/king-papers/documents/interview-meet-press

King, S. (2018, July 14). Colin Kaepernick's forced exile from the NFL has lasted for 500 days. *The Intercept*. Retrieved from www.theintercept.com/2018/07/14/colin-kaepernick-nfl-500-days/

Kivel, P. (1997). *Uprooting racism: How white people can work for racial justice.* Gabriola Island, B.C.: New Society Publishers.

Kohut, H. (1984). *How does analysis cure?* Chicago, IL: University of Chicago Press.

Kopp, S. (1972). *If you meet the Buddha along the road, kill him.* New York, NY: Bantam Books.

Korstad, R., & Leloudis, J. (2010). *To right these wrongs: The North Carolina Fund and the battle to end poverty and inequality in 1960s America.* Chapel Hill, NC: University of North Carolina Press.

Kovel, J. (1970). *White racism: A psychohistory.* New York, NY: Pantheon Books.

Lawrence, C. (1987). The id, the ego, and equal protection: Reckoning with unconscious racism. *Stanford Law Review, 39*(2), 317–388.

Lee, H. (2006). *To kill a mockingbird.* New York, NY: Harper Perennial Modern Classics. (Original work published in 1960)

Lipsitz, G. (1998). *The possessive investment in whiteness: How white people profit from identity politics.* Philadelphia, PA: Temple University Press.

Lockhart, P. R. (2018, September 24). The Dallas police officer who shot Botham Jean has been fired. Vox. Retrieved from www.vox.com/identities/2018/9/24/17896744/amber-guyger-dallas-police-termination-botham-jean

Lorde, A. (1984). *Sister outsider: Essays and speeches.* Berkeley, CA: Crossing Press.

Lukianoff, G., & Haidt, J. (2015, September). The coddling of the American mind. *The Atlantic.* Retrieved from www.theatlantic.com/magazine/archive/2015/09/the-coddling-of-the-american-mind/399356/

Mama, A. (2002). Challenging subjects: Gender, power and identity in African contexts. *The Wellesley Centers for Women Research & Action Report, 23*(2), 6–15. Retrieved from www.wcwonline.org/images/stories/researchandaction/pdf/rar_springsummer2002.pdf

Mate, G. (2003). *When the body says no: Exploring the stress-disease connection.* Hoboken, NJ: John Wiley & Sons.

McIntosh, P. (1988). *White privilege and male privilege: A personal account of coming to see correspondences through work in women's studies* (Working paper No. 189). Wellesley, MA: Wellesley Centers for Women.

Miller, J. B. (1976). *Toward a new psychology of women.* Boston, MA: Beacon Press.

Miller, J. B. (1984). The development of women's sense of self. *Work in Progress, No. 12.* Wellesley, MA: Stone Center Working Paper Series.

Miller, J. B. (1988). Connections, disconnections and violations. *Work in Progress, No. 33.* Wellesley, MA: Stone Center Working Paper Series.

Miller, J. B., & Stiver, I. P. (1995). Relational images and their meanings in psychotherapy. *Work in Progress, No. 47.* Wellesley, MA: Stone Center Working Paper Series.

Miller, J. B., & Stiver, I. P. (1997). *The healing connection: How women form relationships in therapy and in life.* Boston, MA: Beacon Press.

Nhat Hanh, T. (2014). *No mud, no lotus: The art of transforming suffering.* Berkeley, CA: Parallax Press.

Nisbett, R. E., Aronson, J., Blair, C., Dickens, W., Flynn, J., Halpern, D. F., & Turkheimer, E. (2012). Intelligence: New findings and theoretical developments. *American Psychologist, 67*(2), 130–159.

O'Brien, A. (2018). *Suicide rate is up 1.2 percent according to most recent CDC data (year 2016).* Retrieved from afsp.orgsuicide-rate-1-8-percent-according -recent-cdc-data-year-2016/

Parks, S. (2010). *Fierce angels: The strong black woman in American life and culture.* New York, NY: One World/Ballantine Books.

Perls, F. (n.d.). Retrieved from www.gestalttheory.com/quotes/

Perlstein, R. (2012, November 13). *Exclusive: Lee Atwater's infamous 1981 interview on the Southern Strategy.* Retrieved from www.thenation.com/article /exclusive-lee-atwaters-infamous-1981-interview-southern-strategy/

Peters, W. (Producer). (1985, March 26). *A class divided* [Television episode]. *Frontline.* Retrieved from www.pbs.org/wgbh/frontline/film/class-divided/

Phelps, E. A., O'Connor, K. J., Cunningham, W. A., Funayama, E. S., Gatenby, J. C., Gore, J. C., & Banaji, M. R. (2000). Performance on indirect measures of race evaluation predicts amygdala activation. *Journal of Cognitive Neuroscience, 12*(5), 729–738.

Pierce, C. (1974). Psychiatric problems of the black minority. In S. Arieti (Ed.), *American handbook of psychiatry* (pp. 512–523). New York, NY: Basic Books.

Pinderhughes, E. (1989). *Understanding race, ethnicity and power: The key to efficacy in clinical practice.* New York, NY: The Free Press.

Plomin, R. (2018). *Blueprint: How DNA makes us who we are.* London, England: Penguin Books.

Plomin, R., Owen, M. J., & McGuffin, P. (1994). The genetic basis of complex human behaviors. *Science, 264*(5166), 1733–1739.

Popova, M. (n.d.). *The art of "negative capability": Keats on embracing uncertainty and celebrating the mysterious.* Retrieved from www.brainpickings. org/2012/11/01/john-keats-on-negative-capability/

Powery, E. B., & Sadler, R. S., Jr. (2016). *The genesis of liberation: Biblical interpretation in the antebellum narratives of the enslaved.* Louisville, KY: Westminster John Knox Press.

Pratt, R. A. (2002). *We shall not be moved: The desegregation of the University of Georgia.* Athens, GA: University of Georgia Press.

Ransom, J. (2017, August 28). Blacks remain focus of Boston police investigations, searches. *The Boston Globe.* Retrieved from www.bostonglobe.com /metro/2017/08/28/blacks-remain-focus-boston-police-investigations-searches /PDbFr2QZexCEi3zJTO9mOJ/story.html

Robb, C. (2006). *This changes everything: The relational revolution in psychology.* New York, NY: Picador.

Rogers, C. (1965). *Carl Rogers counseling session with Gloria.* Retrieved from www.youtube.com/watch?v=m30jsZx_Ngs

Rumi, J. a. M. (2004). *The essential Rumi* (C. Barks, Trans.). New York, NY: HarperCollins Publishers. (Original work published 1207–1273)

Sanburn, J. (2014, November 25). All the ways Darren Wilson described being afraid of Michael Brown. *Time.* Retrieved from time.com/3605346 /darren-wilson-michael-brown-demon/

Sartre, J. P. (1947, October 18). Americans and their myths: Everything has been said about the United States. *The Nation*. Retrieved from www.thenation.com /article/americans-and-their-myths/

Schafer, R. (1974). Problems in Freud's psychology of women. *Journal of the American Psychoanalytic Association, 22*(3), 459–485.

Schwartz, H. L. (2019). *Connected teaching: Relationships, power, and mattering in higher education*. Sterling, VA: Stylus Publishing.

Slipp, S. (1993). *The Freudian mystique: Freud, women, and feminism*. New York, NY: NYU Press.

Stalvey, L. M. (1970). *The education of a WASP*. Madison, WI: The University of Wisconsin Press.

Steele, C. M. (2010). *Whistling Vivaldi: How stereotypes affect us and what we can do*. New York, NY: W. W. Norton & Co.

Stiver, I. P. (1990). A relational approach to therapeutic impasses. *Work in Progress, No. 58*. Wellesley, MA: Stone Center Working Paper Series.

Stiver, I. P. (2004). Therapist authenticity. In J. Jordan, M. Walker, & L. Hartling (Eds.), *The complexity of connection: Writings from the Stone Center's Jean Baker Miller Training Institute* (pp. 72–75). New York, NY: Guilford Press.

Sue, D. W. (Ed.). (2010). *Microaggressions and marginality: Manifestations, dynamics, and impact*. Hoboken, NJ: John Wiley & Sons.

Sue, D. W. (2015). *Race talk and the conspiracy of silence: Understanding and facilitating difficult dialogues on race*. Hoboken, NJ: John Wiley & Sons.

Sue, D. W., Alsaidi, S., Awad, M. N., Glaeser, E., Calle, C. Z., & Mendez, N. (2019). Disarming racial microaggressions: Microintervention strategies for targets, White allies, and bystanders. *American Psychologist, 74*(1), 128–142.

Tatum, B. D. (1993). Racial identity development and relational theory: The case of black women in white communities. *Work in Progress, No. 63*. Wellesley, MA: Stone Center Working Paper Series.

Tatum, B. D. (2018, November). Cultural competence: A day of learning, leading, and leaning in. Presentation at professional development seminar for Needham Public Schools, Needham, MA.

Thomas, A., & Sillen, S. (1972). *Racism and psychiatry*. New York, NY: Brunner Routledge.

Thomas, K. R. (2008). Macrononsense in multiculturalism. *American Psychologist, 63*(4), 274–275.

Turkheimer, E. (2000). Three laws of behavior genetics and what they mean. *Current Directions in Psychological Science, 9*(5), 160–164.

U. S. Department of Education, Office for Civil Rights. (2018, April). *2015–16 Civil rights data collection: School climate and safety*. Retrieved from www2.ed.gov /about/offices/list/ocr/docs/school-climate-and-safety.pdf

van der Kolk, B. (2014). *The body keeps the score: Brain, mind, and body in the healing of trauma*. New York, NY: Viking.

Walker, M. (1999). Race, self and society: Relational challenges in a culture of disconnection. *Work in Progress, No. 85*. Wellesley, MA: Stone Center Working Paper Series.

Walker, M. (2004). Walking a piece of the way: Race, power, and therapeutic movement. In M. Walker, & W. B. Rosen (Eds.), *How connections heal: Stories from relational-cultural therapy* (pp. 36–52). New York, NY: Guilford Press.

Walker, M. (2005). Critical thinking: Developmental myths, stigmas, and stereotypes. In D. Comstock (Ed.), *Diversity and development: Critical contexts that
shape our lives and relationships* (pp. 47–66). Belmont, CA: Brooks/Cole.

Walker, M. (2010). What's a feminist therapist to do? Engaging the relational paradox in a post-feminist culture. *Women & Therapy, 34*(1–2), 38–58.

Walker, M. (2012). Getting to the truths about race: Reflections on the politics of
connection in *The Help*. *Work in Progress, No. 109*. Wellesley, MA: Stone Center Working Paper Series.

Walker, M., & Miller, J. B. (2000). Racial images and relational possibilities. *Talking
Paper No. 2*, Wellesley, MA: Stone Center Publication.

Walker, M., & Rosen, W. B. (Eds.). (2004). *How connections heal: Stories from
relational-cultural therapy*. New York, NY: Guilford Press.

Wexler, B. E. (2006). *Brain and culture: Neurobiology, ideology, and social change*.
Cambridge, MA: MIT Press.

Wheatley, M. J. (2002). *Turning to one another: Simple conversations to restore
hope to the future*. San Francisco, CA: Berrett-Koehler Publishers.

Wise, T. (2008). *Speaking treason fluently: Anti-racist reflections from an angry
white male*. Brooklyn, NY: Soft Skull Press.

Wise, T. (2011). *White like me: Reflections on race from a privileged son*. Berkeley,
CA: Soft Skull Press.

Zinn, H. (2015). *A people's history of the United States*. New York, NY: Harper
Perennial. (Original work published 2003)

Index

About the Author

Maureen Walker is a licensed psychologist, educator, and writer whose work is devoted to helping people bridge cultural differences such as race, religion, gender, and other social status markers.

Born in Augusta, Georgia, during the period of legally mandated racial segregation, she attended segregated, underresourced public schools. In spite of the lack of resources, her love of learning was nurtured by women and men who considered teaching a sacred duty to spark the ambitions and cultivate the talents of their students. Upon graduation from high school, she entered Mercer University and graduated with degrees in vocal performance and English. Immediately after graduation, she began teaching in Georgia public schools where de jure segregation had ended but many of the norms of the Old South persisted. Although her formal role was teaching English literature to high school students, she was equally committed to helping young people of all races navigate the complexities of evolving cultural realities. While working, she returned to Mercer University to obtain a master's degree in education and began a program of study in business administration.

After 8 years in public education, Maureen accepted a position as executive director of a women's center. While serving in this capacity, she entered a doctoral program in counseling psychology, earning her PhD with a clinical concentration in psychotherapy from Georgia State University. In 1991, she started work as a staff psychologist in the MBA Counseling Service at Harvard Business School. During her career at Harvard, she served in various roles, retiring after 25 years as the Director of Student Support Services.

Concurrent with her work at Harvard, Maureen has maintained private clinical practice in psychotherapy in Cambridge, Massachusetts, since 1993. At the International Center for Growth in Connection (formerly known as the Jean Baker Miller Institute), she provides training and supervision to students and practitioners of relational-cultural theory. In addition to coediting two books on relational-cultural psychotherapy, she has authored textbook chapters, journal articles, and numerous papers in the Wellesley College Stone Center Works in Progress Series.

She is supported in her life work by a spiritual, intellectual, and fun-filled partnership with her husband, Bill Larkin; her two big-hearted and talented children, Angela Shenk and Walker Sands; and her four beloved grandchildren.